W.H. Strobridge

Catalogue of a collection of ancient and modern coins

W.H. Strobridge

Catalogue of a collection of ancient and modern coins

ISBN/EAN: 9783741139628

Manufactured in Europe, USA, Canada, Australia, Japa

Cover: Foto ©ninafisch / pixelio.de

Manufactured and distributed by brebook publishing software (www.brebook.com)

W.H. Strobridge

Catalogue of a collection of ancient and modern coins

PREFACE.

A few words of explanation and apology are needed here.

A due regard to order in a work like this, would require such an arrangement of its materials as would enable the reader to survey at one view, and under a single head, every article of each particular class described therein.

But the exigencies of the professional compiler of coin catalogues often forbid such a classification; the different properties placed in his hands requiring to be kept apart, regardless of congruity.

To prevent *greater* confusion, a division of the catalogue into parts—as in the present instance—is sometimes resorted to; by which arrangement, the principal collections can be separately referred to, while in the addendas small parcels following each other, with their inevitable repetitions, will be more readily excused.

Part I. is devoted to a classification and brief description of a cabinet of Ancient and Modern Coins, already known here as the "Havana Collection."

The strength of this collection lies in its stores of the Coins of Spain, and the colonies of that country in the new world.

Spain, or Iberia—as the Spanish Peninsula was once called—was early colonized by nations from the East, and later by the Carthaginians and Romans. Innumerable coins exist with Phœnician, Greek, and Punic inscriptions, as well as with Celtiberian and Roman legends. The Celtiberian Alphabet is a mixture of the older writing of the Phœnicians and Greeks with native and Carthaginian letters.

Numismatists do not allow that the great bulk of these coins are older than the second century before Christ, but those with Greek and Phœnician inscriptions may have a much higher antiquity. After the conquest of the country by the Romans, the date of the coins may be easily fixed, the head of the Emperor being always found on them; and even before the Roman power became settled, Latin legends betray an increasing Roman influence dating from the time of the Carthaginian war.

There has been no considerable number of these coins within easy reach of American collectors until now.

This division of the collection was sufficiently full to allow of its being catalogued in lots of six, and frequently more, pieces. This has been done with a view to avoid tediousness at the sale; it will also prove advantageous to the collector, as there are but few duplicates, and care has been taken to secure variety in each lot.

The collection was made by a SPANIARD, and his *amor patriæ* has evidently guided his selection. Equally with the Ancient, the coins of Modern Spain, in gold and silver of large size, deserve especial mention and praise. There are nearly half a hundred of Isabella and Ferdinand, and the number and quality of the " Proclamation " pieces are quite unprecedented.

There are also many unusually fine and rare pieces to be found among the Coins and Medals of England, examples of which are: No. 457, Penny of Edgar ; No. 472, Crown of Edward VI.; No. 482, Medal of Cromwell ; No. 483, Medal by *Simon ;* Nos. 488, 490, and 492, *uncirculated* Half Crowns of James II., William and Mary, and William III.; No. 538, Farthing of Anna ; etc., etc.

Part II. is the property of a gentleman still in the field as a collector. The purchase of a cabinet with a large number of duplicates, caused the amalgamated stock of new and old Coins to require this extensive depletion to bring it into reasonable proportions. There are fine Silver Medals in this division, and a large number of moderately fine U. S. and foreign Silver Coins.

In the addenda to Part I. there are a number of uncirculated and extremely fine Dollars and Half Dollars; and in the second addenda, some of the best Coins in the catalogue. In this division will be found a line of Proof Sets and other pieces left by the late Colin Lightbody, among them an uncirculated 1797 half-dime; a cent of 1809, uncommonly fine; and a rare Canadian token of Louis XV. Following Mr. Lightbody's coins are a number of uncirculated Polish and Russian Silver coins from the Stenz Collection.

The large number of Ancient Coins in this catalogue, massed in lots of twenty and more pieces, may reasonably be expected to give a new impulse to their acquisition and study—a study which the celebrated Mionnet has called, "*une magnifique branche d'archéologie.*"

WILLIAM H. STROBRIDGE.

CLINTON HALL, *Sept.* 12, 1876.

CATALOGUE OF COINS.

PART I.

COPPER COINS OF ANCIENT HISPANIA.

[*Arranged according to* WELLENHEIM, *the numbers referring to his catalogue, and the scale of rarity agreeing with his.*]

SPAIN (in general).

1 HEAD without beard; rev. horsemen to r., some with Phœnician legends, others with Latin. 1st and 2d size. Poor, rare.   6 pieces
2 Similar lot.   6 "
3 Similar; all 2d size.   6 "
4 Similar to last.   6 "
5 Another; same.   6 "
6 CELTIBERIAN. Various types, but all differing from those before described. 2d size; poor.   6 pieces
7 Similar; poor, but uncommon.   6 "
8 Similar; same description.   6 "
9 Various Celtiberian.   6 "

Lusitania.

10 BALSA. Bare head to r.; rev. bull to r. (No. 3). Poor, with others (Roman Colonial), good lot.   6 pieces
11 EMERITA. Head of Augustus to l.; rev. front of a temple with two towers united by an arch; varieties, no duplicates. 2d size, good lot.   6 pieces

12 EMERITA. 1st and 2d size; Augustus and other Emperors.
6 pieces
13 —— Another lot. 6 "
14 —— Head of Augustus to l.; rev. P. CARISIVS - LEG AVGVSTI. Well. No. 4. 2d size, with others (Roman Colonial); rare. 6 pieces

Baetica.

15 ABDERA. Head of Cæsar?; rev. a temple tetrastyle with others. 2d and 3d size; poor. 6 pieces
16 ACINIPO. ACINIPO between two ears of barley; rev. bunch of grapes. 2d size; fair lot; R 3. 6 pieces
17 AMBA (not in Well.). Head; in field, hand; rev. Centaur, in field, star, with others. 2d and 3d size; poor, very rare. 6 pieces
18 ARIA. Head to r.; rev. horseman with lance and Celtiberian legend (not according to Well., but on another authority). 2d size; fair lot, rare. 6 pieces
19 Another lot. 6 "
20 ASIDO. Bare head to r.; rev. bull and crescent, on others a star; Celtiberian leg. 3d size; well preserved and remarkable. 6 pieces
21 Similar of Asido; others of Acinipo and Aria. 6 "
22 CAURA (not in Well.). Head to r.; rev. CAVRA. above, large fish; other Celtiberian; poor. 6 pieces
23 CARMO. Head casqued to r. within a crown of myrtle; rev. between two ears of barley .CARMO. 1st size. Mionnet 1-S-41: Well. 21. Well preserved, R. 3.
24 Others. 1st and 2d size; poor. 6 pieces
25 CARTEIA. Turreted female head; rev. Neptune standing, with one foot on a rock, in his hand, trident and dolphin'; same head; rev. rudder; same; rev. Cupid on a dolphin, etc., etc. Fine and rare lot. 6 pieces
26 Similar lot. 6 "
27 Another lot; fair. 6 "
28 Similar. 8 "
29 CARISA (not in Well.). Bare head; rev. vase. 3d size; fair. 6 pieces
30 CORDUBA. Head of Venus to r.; rev. Cupid standing, with torch and cornucopia, and two other types described by Well., No. 36 to 39. 2d and 3d size; fair, rare. 6 pieces
31 Similar lot. 6 "
32 Another lot, with implements of worship and sacrifice.
6 pieces

Copper Coins of Ancient Hispania. 3

33 CANACA. Head of Hercules; rev. two fish and Phœn. legend, and others of Corduba. Very fine lot. 5 pieces
34 GADES. Head of Hercules; rev. two fish, several varieties not described elsewhere, *e. g.*, Hercules with club before his face; some with a single fish. Fine. 6 pieces
35 Another of this place; 2d and 3d size. 6 "
36 Similar lot. 6 "
37 Another, similar. 10 "
38 A mixed lot of Celtiberian; poor. 10 "
39 ILIPA. ILIPENSE between two lines, below, a large fish; rev. ear of barley. Two sizes. 6 pieces
40 IRIPPO. Bare head to r. IRIPPO; rev. female seated, in r. hand, pineapple; in l. horn of plenty. 2d size; fine. R. 3. Well. 46.
41 ⸺ Varieties of same type; fair lot and rare. 6 pieces
42 Others attributed to this place, with similar head; on rev an animal and crescent. 2d size. 6 pieces
43 ITALICA. *Augustus;* obv. PERM.AVG-MVNIC-ITALIC bare head of Augustus to r.; rev. Rome standing, in r. hand hasta and parazonium; in left, a shield. 1st size, fair. R. 2, Well. 47. Others of Augustus, one with cavalier to r., under the horse ITALIC; one with eagle and standards. All 1st size; rather poor, but uncommon and interesting. 6 pieces
44 ⸺ Tiberius and Brutus, on each a head; rev. altar with ins. | PROVID -ENTIAE AVGVSTI, | and eagle between two ensigns. 1st and 2d size. R. 2 and 4, Well. 49 and 51. Fair to fine. 6 pieces
45 ITUCI. Cavalier armed; rev. two ears of barley. 2d size; poor; R. 3, Well. 52, and three others attributed to the same province (not in Well.). 6 pieces
46 ⸺ Others, both types; all poor, but very rare. 8 "
47 LAELIA (not in Well.). LAELIA between two branches of palm; rev. cavalier with lance, with others similar and different types; poor. 6 pieces
48 LASTIGI. Helmeted head within myrtle crown; rev. LAS in similar crown; small brass, well preserved. Well. 53, R. 6, with others larger, not in Well., with LASTIGI between two lines; on each side a head of barley. Larger size, and undoubtedly still more rare. 3 pieces
49 OBULCO. Rude female head to r. OBVLCO; rev. Celtiberian ins. in two lines, between an ear of barley and an implement not understood. 1st size. Varieties same type. Well. 58. 6 pieces

50 OLONT (not in Well.). Female head; rev. Cavalier, below the horse OLONT; others with a tree. Very rare. 3d size. 5 pieces

51 OSSET. Beardless head to r. OSSET; rev. man standing naked, holding in r. hand a bunch of grapes. Varieties 2d second size. From good to poor. R. 2, Well 67. 6 pieces

52 ROMULA; Augustus and Livia. Radiated head of Augustus to r. COL. ROM. PERM-DIVI-AVG; rev. head of Livia poised on a globe to l. IVLIA-AVGVSTA-GENETRIX-ORBIS. 1st size and well preserved. R. 6, Well. No. 69.

53 Duplicate of this rare coin, nearly as fine.

54 SACILI. Laureated head to r.; rev. horse stepping to r. Poor. R. 6, Well. 73; others attributed to this place, with horse on rev. 6 pieces

55 SESTI (?). Head of Hercules to l.; rev. two fishes and crescent; Phœnician legend (not in Well.). 1st and 2d size. Good lot. 6 pieces

56 TRADUCTA (JULIA). Head of Augustus to l. PERM-CAES-AVG.; rev. within a crown of oak, JVLIA-TRAD. Well. 77. 2d size. 6 pieces

57 —— Similar lot. 6 pieces

58 —— Others, Jul. Trad., with duplicates of No. 52 and No. 51. 6 pieces

59 URSO. Diademed head; rev. Sphinx; ins. Celt. 1st size. R. 3, Well. 79. Fair. Varieties. 2 pieces

60 —— Others; same type. 2 "

Tarraconensis.

61 BIBILIS. Head to r. dolphins; rev. Celtiberian inscription and horseman armed with a lance. Well. 90. 1st size. Fair, R. One same size, with head of Augustus; rev. Cavalier BILBILIS. Another with II.VIR within wreath, and other varieties. A rare lot. 6 pieces

62 CÆSAR-AUGUSTA. Laureated head of Augustus. IMP. AVGVSTVS. TRIB. POTES. XX; rev. a Priest tracing the limits of a colony with a plough drawn by two oxen. CAES-AVGVS-CN-DOM-AMP-C-VET-LANC-II-VIR. Varieties of this type. 1st size. Fair to poor, rare. 6 pieces

63 —— Others of Augustus for this colony. 1st and 2d size. Rather poor. 6 pieces

64 CÆSAR Augustus and Tiberius. 1st and 2d size. Reverse of Oxen—a bull—and military standards. Rare lot, in fine preservation. 6 pieces
65 —— with two and three heads of the Cæsars, and other types. 6 pieces
66 —— Small brass of this colony. 6 "
67 CALAGURRIS-JULIA (not in Well.) Head of Augustus; rev. bull to r. 1. NER. FES. and one of Calagurris Nassica. 1st size. Poor. 4 pieces
68 CATHARGO-NOVA. Head of Augustus; rev. Labyrinth, round form. 1st size. Fair pres. and R. 4, Well. 126.
69 —— Heads of Nero and Drusus on the rev. of a coin of Tiberius. Well. 125, R 4. Fair. 2 pieces
70 —— Same as 68, and one with heads of Caius and Lucius. (R 4). Other rare types. 4 pieces
71 CASCANTUM. Head of Augustus; rev. a bull; below, CAS-CANTVM. 2d size R 4. Well. 133. 2 pieces
72 CELSA. Young beardless head, around, 3 dolphins; no ins.; rev. a cavalier carrying a palm over his shoulder; ins. Celtiberian; large 1st brass. Well. 134. A noble coin, in good preservation. Rare.
73 —— Head of Augustus; rev. bull to r. L-BACCIO-M-FESTO-II VIR C-X-I CEL. Well. 139. Well preserved and patinated, with other types of the Cavalier. Fair to poor. 6 pieces
74 —— Young head, with ivy fillet (young Bacchus?), around, 3 dolphins; rev. same as 72. 2 fine. Others.
4 pieces
75 CLUNIA. Head of Tiberius; rev. bull to l. Well. 159. 2d size. Poor, with some Emporiae, and others.
6 pieces
76 DERTOSA. *Tiberius* and *Augustus;* head of the former laureated; rev. radiated head of Augustus. Fine. 2d size. Well. 161, R. 6.
77 EMPORIAE. Head of Ceres; rev. Pegasus. Various types. Good lot. 4 pieces
78 HELMANTICA. Bearded head to r.; rev. cavalier with lance. Celtiberian ins. Fine. Well. 179. 3 pieces
79 ILERCAVONIA. Head of Tiberius; rev. a vessel under full sail. ILERCAVONIA-DERT (for Dertosa). 2d size. Fine and R. 4, Well. 189.
80 ILERDA. Head of Augustus; rev. wolf. ILERDA. One with barbarus head; Celt. ins. Rare. 3 pieces

81 ILICI. Head of Augustus; rev. Temple of Juno, with one of Lucifera, and others. 2d size. 6 pieces
82 LUCIFERAE-FANUM; obv. head of Vulcan, behind forceps; rev. head of Venus, front face, with rays. See Well. No. 54, etc. R. 3. 2d size. Fair condition. 6 pieces
83 OSICERDA. Head; rev. horseman to r., with lance; Celt. ins. (Well. 209); on others, bull; on some, elephant. (Doubtful.) Poor. 6 pieces
84 SAETABIS (or Saetabi). Head of Hercules to r., behind, club; rev. horseman to r., with palm; Celt. ins. (Well. 215). 1st size. Patinated and fine. Others with bull to r. Various sizes. Ordinary. 6 pieces
85 —— Another lot. 6 "
86 SAGUNTUM. Old head; rev. horseman; Celt. ins.; Shell; rev. dolphin's head; rev. prow of a ship. Compare with Well. Different sizes. Fair lot. Rare.
87 —— Another; similar lot. 6 pieces
88 —— Repetition of last. 10 "
89 SEGOBRIGA. Head between two dolphins; rev. horseman, with lance, Celteberian ins.; Tiberius; rev. SEGOBRIGA within wreath of oak; one with horseman, below the horse, SEGOBRIGA. Rare lot. 6 pieces
90 SEGOVIA AND TETELSIS; with others already described. 10 pieces
91 TARRACO. Head laureated; rev. octostyle temple; others with heads of Augustus and Tiberius, etc. 6 pieces
92 TURIASO AND VALENTIA. Head of Tiberius laureated; rev. MARSO — C – MARI – VEGETO – II – VIR. Bull to r. (Well. 252), and head; rev. thunderbolt and cornucopia. 6 pieces
93 VARIOUS Celtiberian coins. 10 pieces
94 Similar lot. 10 pieces
95 SPANISH, Gallic, and some from North of Africa, all kindred coins. Rare and interesting lot. 10 pieces
96 FINE Coin of Brundusium. Head of Neptune; rev. Amphion on a dolphin, lyre in hand, BRVN. One of Cleopatra, Queen of Egypt; her portrait; rev. Cupid. One of Vabalathus (son of Zenobia), and others equally interesting. 10 pieces
97 Indifferent lot of 10 pieces
98 Better selection, good lot. 10 pieces
99 CELTIBERIA, Mauretania, and Parthian coins. 6 pieces

Silver Coins of Ancient Hispania. 7

Continuation of Spanish Coins, from the earliest times down to the reign of Alfonso XII. In silver when not otherwise defined; authorities followed, Aloiss Heiss & Wellenheim's Catalogue.

100 Saetabi (Tarraconensis). Beardless old head, short curly hair, behind, some symbol, as ◯- * ☾-; rev. horseman at full speed; Celtiberian ins.; drachma in beautiful preservation. 3 pieces

101 Three others, same province, very good.

102 Liuva I. (567, 572). Bust in helmet, above a square with the sign of the crose, ILIAVA ILLVZTI; rev. Victory seated. Fine GOLD coin, size of the silver penny; very rare. (Not in Well.) Compare with No. 61 of that catalogue. Valuable.

103 Sanchez III. 1157-58. Bust to r., SANCIVS REX; rev. cross, with two limbs, etc. Penny; compare with Well. 293, R R R. Very fine.

104 Alphonso 8th. (1158-96). Silver money (groat size), and Henry 1st, Anno 1214; same size, the latter with crowned bust; rev. cross, ENRICVS REX CASTEL, etc. R R. 2 pieces

105 Alphonso 9th (1218), and Sanchez IV. (1284-1295.) Well. 296, R R. Silver pennies. 2 pieces

106 Peter I. 1350-1368. PETRVS-REX-CASTELLE E - LEGIONIS, lion; rev. castle. Splendid groat, half groats (2), and penny. R R. Compare with Well. 298. 4 pieces

107 Henry II. 1368-1379. Groats; one with bust to the waist, full face (base); one with arms of Castile and Leon; rev. inscription in two circles and monogram (fine silver), and two small coins, base. Well. R R. 4 pieces

108 Henry III., 1390-1406; John I. (1379). Silver coin (groat size), bust crowned; rev. cross, annulet, and three pellets in angles. Crowned monogram; rev. Agnus Dei, half-groat size, and pennies. 4 pieces

109 John II., 1407; and Henry IV. (1454). On the former (a penny) bust in profile; rev. castle on the last (groats), crowned bust full face; rev. castle; base, one pierced, RR.; (on these Groats the legend runs, ENRICVS - QVARTVS - DEI - GRAT. See Well. 302). Valuable lot. 5 pieces

110 Other billon Groats of Henry IV., RR.; fine. 3 pieces

111 Alphonso V. (of Portugal), and Henry IV., billon and copper money. Valuable. 3 pieces

8 *Silver Coins of Ancient Hispania.*

1.25 — 112 FERDINAND AND ISABELLA, (Ferd. V. the Catholic, and Isabella I.), 1474-1516; obv. arms of Leon, Castile, Aragon, Sicily and Granada crowned. FERNANDVS ET ELISABET; rev. a yoke and bundle of arrows. REX ET REGINA CASTELE LEGIONIS, a piece of 2 Reals (¼ Doll.), has become perfectly oxidized and black, but sharp as when struck; rare to excess. See Heiss, 78; not in Well.

3.00 — 113 —— Similar piece of one Real (Quarter Dollar), bright and sharp as last; rare.

1.50 — 114 —— Variety of same type. Equally fine.

.75 — 115 —— Another variety. Dark and fine real.

4.00 — 116 —— Real, FERNANDVS ET HELISA. Arms as before; rev. REX ET REGINA - CAST - LEON - DG. Yoke and bundle of arrows; thinner than last. Extremely fine and rare.

1.50 — 117 —— Another. Slight variety. Equally fine.

.40 — 118 —— Real and half do.; on the last, arrows on one side, yoke on the rev.; very fine. 2 pieces

" — 119 —— Repetition of last, Real and half do. 2 pieces

.47 — 120 —— Same. 2 pieces

.30 — 121 —— Varieties of same. 2 pieces

.40 — 122 —— Real like last, and one of Ferdinand V. 2 pieces

3.2² — 123 —— A double ducat struck in lead, entirely black with age, and different from any engraved by *Heiss*. It has the busts of Ferdinand and Isabella face to face, with the usual legend. On the rev. are the yoke and arrows instead of the shield and coat-of-arms usually found on their gold coins. With this, a selection of copper and *billon* coins, all described in Heiss' work. The condition of each piece very fine; a desirable lot. 6 pieces

.15 — 124 —— Similar lot, without the double ducat; interesting. 8 pieces

1.00 — 125 CHARLES I. AND JUANA (Charles V. as Emperor of Germ.), 1516-1565. Half-dollar; obv. on a crowned shield, the arms of Castile Leon and Granada, CAROLVS ET JOANA REGS; rev. two pillars crowned, rising from the sea; leg. PLV—SVL—TRA; below, 4. Oxidized and black, but very sharp; very rare. See Heiss, No. 6, Pl. 32.

9c — 126 —— Real of this type, with a half-real, having a large K°I in the field (for Karolus and Joana). The first extremely fine, and both rare; with these a quarter-dollar medal, with the pillars relating to the New World, and found only on coins made from American silver (as I am informed and believe). 3 pieces

Silver Coins of Ancient Hispania. 9

127 PHILIP II. 1556–1598. A number of rare coins (real and half-real size), and a copper jeton. 8 pieces

128 PHILIP III. 1598–1621. Extremely fine silver coins, with his bust; rev. cross, annulets, and balls in the angles. Eighth and sixteenth dolls., 2 of each. 4 pieces

129 —— A cut half-dollar, with the reverse of last, including the Jerusalem cross; rare.

130 A number of Early Spanish coins not classified, many with rude heads; a desirable lot, from groat to penny size; all well preserved. 24 pieces

131 Similar, not as fine. 20 "

132 PHILIP IIII. 1621–1665. Irregular shaped coins, cut and hammered planchets; prototypes of the well known "Cob money;" a dollar, black with age, and a 17 real piece (quarter-dollar) with his bust, dated 1643. 4 pieces

133 CHARLES II. 1665 to 1700. Coins of the value of pistareens and half do (2 and 4). 6 pieces

[Some of these with the cypher of Maria, are rare.]

134 PHILIP V. 1700–1746. Dollar of Mexico and 4 pistareens. (Int. value, $1.80.) 5 pieces

135 —— Cob money; 2 reals and smaller. 10 "

136 LOUIS I. 1724. Pistareens; rare. 2 "

137 FERDINAND VI. 1746–1759. Proc. medal on his coronation (half-doll.); one, 1747, *cast* in Cuba, smaller, very rare; dollar of 1758; pierced, but rare. 3 pieces

138 CHARLES III. 1759–1788. Proc. half-doll. (American) uncirculated quarter, and dollar of Mexico, pierced. 3 pieces

139 —— Quarters (7), pistareens (2), eighths (3), and sixteenths (3). (Int. value, $2.68.) 14 pieces

140 CHARLES IV. 1788–1808. Pillar dollars, 1789–1794 and and 1802; very fine. 3 pieces

141 —— Shilling; extremely fine, rare.

142 FERDINAND VII. 1808–1833. Dollar 1816, Mexican mint, fine; and one of Zacatecas (Mo.), rare. 2 pieces

143 —— Another dollar of Zacatecas; rev. cross on a mountain, below, L.V.O. Very fine, rare.

144 —— Quarter of Zacatecas, better than usually found, and others of Spain; different types; two very fine. 6 pcs

145 —— Eighth-dollar; one uncir. 4 pieces

146 —— Gen. Vargas' dollar of 1812; rev. CAXADE SOMBRETE-CM counterstamped on shield with Spanish arms; good example, rare.

10   *Silver Coins of Ancient Hispania.*

1,40 147 FERDINAND VII. Dollar and half-dollar of Gen. Vargas, the latter with counterstamp (rare to excess, not even noticed by Heiss); good examples.   2 pieces
1.10 148 —— Manila, 1828, dollar; restruck Peruvian dollar. Heiss Pl. 67, No. 74. Fine and very rare.
175 149 —— Barcelona. Siege dollar (5 PESETAS) of 1810; rev. arms on a diamond-shaped shield within circle of oak leaves and acorns formed into a wreath; edge engrailed; uncirculated; in this condition rare.
55 150 —— Half-dollar of same type.
212 151 —— Balearian Islands dollar of 1523; obv. FERN 7°-P-LA-G-D-DIOS-Y-LA-CONST around the arms of *Mallorca?* 5-P; rev. within laurel wreath, YSLAS BALEARES-1823; a fine border around the circumference. Heiss, 52. Fine and rare.
212 152 —— Another, same as last.
220 153 —— Triplicate, equally fine.
137 154 —— Siege dollar of 1821, "30 sous;" rev. SALVS - POPVLA counterstamped; below, the same arms, Mallorca (Catalonia?). Very fine, scarce.
" 155 —— Duplicate, equally fine.
50¢ 156 —— Half-dollar; head within two circles of pearls; rev. within wreath of laurel RESELLADO. Heiss, No. 38, Pl. 65. Good example, rare.
90 157 —— Quarter-dollars of Valencia; rev. VALSITIADA
22½   POR LOS ENEMIGOS DE LA LIBERTAD, arms of Valencia crowned; on each side, letter L and 4 - R. Some are siege pieces, and very rare; various dates, with slight differences in legend and design; one struck in tin; all very fine.   5 pieces
90 158 ISABELLA II. 1833–1868. Dollars of 1855, '58, '61, and '67; 2 uncir., and half-dollar of 1855.   5 pieces
27² 159 —— Brilliant uncirculated quarters, various dates and styles; no duplicates.   4 pieces
m² 160 —— Other quarter-dollars.   6   "
12 161 —— Dimes or 2 reals (eighth-dollars).   3   "
175 162 REPUBLIC. Dollar of 1870; fine, scarce.
38 163 AMADEUS I. Dollar of 1871; fine, scarce.
" 164 ALFONSO XII. 1875. Uncir. dollar; scarce.

Acclamation Coins and a few Medals in honor of Spanish Sovereigns—Silver.

212 165 CHARLES III. Merit or Prize Medal by *Peleguer*, fine bust; rev. the province of Valencia bestowing a prize. Dollar size; very fine, rare.
55 166 —— Another Premium Medal, nearly as large.

Acclamation Coins, etc., Silver. 11

1,00 167 CHARLES IV. Dollar Medal, 1790, bust; rev. cross on a mountain, ME FERE-JAM-TOTVM, etc.; pierced, but ex. fine.

6 0 168 —— 1796. Busts of the King and Queen; rev. equestrian statue and ins.; pierced, very fine; nearly dollar size.

5 5 169 —— Cast Medal, 1787; rev. a fortress with two towers, standing on the sea; MICAEL. NUNES-GVANAVACO. Nearly dollar size; similar medal of 1789, smaller. 2 pieces

2 5 170 —— Acclamation Coins of the quarter-dollar size, 1789 and '90; uncommonly fine. 4 pieces

2 0 171 —— Similar lot, not as fine. 4 pieces

3 2 172 —— Cast Medalets (Havana) and Acclamation eighth-dollars. 4 pieces

2.00 173 FERDINAND VII. Busts of the King and Queen; rev. "Hispan et Lusitan foldees," etc.; man (Hercules?) nearly nude, holding two lions between the pillars of Hercules. Nearly dollar size, A.D. 1816; very fine, rare.

9 0 174 —— Duplicate of last, with another of same size, with the Castle of San Juan de Ulluoa, 1825; a cast medal, and remarkably fine. 2 pieces

3 5 175 —— Acclamation quarters of 1808; Guatemala, Mexico, Truxillo, and Madrid. *Extremely* fine; a beautiful lot. 4 pieces

3 0 176 —— Similar for San Salvador, Guatemala, Mexico, Santander, etc. Not equal to last; some pierced. 8 pieces

2 0 177 —— Acclamation pieces of half the size of last (eighth-doll.) Rare and fine lot. 4 pieces

1 2 178 —— Others of this size; some of previous kings, and others of Iturbide, Emp. of Mexico. Ordinary lot. 10 pieces

6 5 179 ISABELLA II. Cast Allegiance Medals of Trinidad (Alejo Isnaga), 1834; half-dollar size, and two smaller. Very remarkable productions, and undoubtedly rare. 4 pcs

5 0 180 —— Beautiful proof medals of the quarter-dollar size, in honor of her accession in 1834, by *Picard* and others. "Santiago de las begas," "Guanabaco," "Iaruco," "Santa Maria del Rosario," "Mallorca," Matanzas. Superb lot. 6 pieces

3 0 181 —— Another lot of the same size and quality. ("

" 182 —— A selection similar and hardly inferior; all very fine. 6 pieces

2 7 2 183 —— Medalets on thick planchets, of extremely fine work, and all uncirculated, commemorating important events in Spain; larger than last. 6 pieces

1 7 2 184 —— Another lot same size, equally fine. 6 "

Spanish Coins in Gold.

25   185 ISABELLA II. Acclamation pieces of one real (eighth-doll.); beautiful proofs, *rare to excess.*   6 pieces
18   186 —— Similar, and of same quality.   6 "
10   187 —— Similar, some pierced; inferior to last.   6 "
25   188 —— Larger medals, 2 half-dollar size; worn and pierced.   6 pieces
110   189 SILVER MEDAL of the "Reg. Coll. Soc. Jesu."; rev. "Religioni et Bonis Artibus." Doll. size, proof.
"   190 —— "Facultád de Filosofia;" same size, fine.
"   191 —— On the introduction of Gas into Havana in 1857; beautiful proof, doll. size.
100   192 —— Donna Antonia Dominguez, "Condesa De San Antonia," NACID EN LA HABANA, 6 Nov., 1860; doll. size, fine proof.
220   193 —— Duplicate of last, with prize medal; same size and quality. ("El Licco de la Habana Presnia el Merito.")   2 pieces
8c   194 —— To commemorate the erection of a statue in honor of COLUMBUS in Cardenas, 19th Nov., 1862; thick oval medal, size 22 x 26; fine and rare.
700   195 —— Spain to the brave who fell in defense of her rights in Cuba, awarded in 1875; a diamond-shaped shield, garnished by a wreath without, and surmounted by a crown; on one side, Spain seated; rev. ins.; including loop, 3 inches long; rare.
100   196 —— Charles IV.; rev. SOLVTIS CAELESTI NVMINI VOTIS, 1786. (1½ oz.) Very good condition.
87   197 —— Isabella II. A LA TNVICTA BALBAO, etc.; rev. Queen and Princess standing; very fine. (1 oz.)
11   198 BAPTISMAL and other silver medalets, and a beautiful shilling (eighth-doll.) of Charles III.   9 pieces
11   199 ACCLAMATION and other Spanish coins of the "sixteenth" size; very fine.   6 pieces
8   200 —— Similar lot, pierced.   10 "

Spanish Coins Continued.
Gold.

7 25   201 PHILIP V. Doubloon (8 Marks), 1745; mailed bust to r.; rev. shield crowned and encircled with the collar of the Order of the Cross of Esperitu Santo. Very fine, rare.
8 50   202 —— Half-doubloon (4 M.), same type; very fine, rare.
20   203 —— Eighth do (1 M.), same; pierced.   2 pieces
17 25   204 FERDINAND VI. Doubloon, 1753; same type as No. 201 (8 M.), very fine.

Coins of Portugal and Brazil. 13

205 FERDINAND VI. A variety, doubloon without the "8 M.," and on the collar, the cross hanging below the golden fleece, 1754; very fine, rare.
206 —— Half-doubloon, 1757; rev. shield crowned; very fine.
207 —— Eighth-doubloon, same type, 1753; very fine.
210 CHARLES III. Two Marks, quarter-doubloon of 1760; very rare, ordinary.
211 —— Sixteenth-doubloon, half-mark. 2 pieces
212 —— Mark (eighth-doubloon), 1770; very fine.
213 JOSEPH NAPOLEON. 1809. Piece of 80 reals (of 5 cts. each), quarter-doubloon; uncirculated, very rare.
214 FERDINAND VII. Doubloon (8 scudi) of 1820, bust; rev. arms crowned, collar of the Order of the Golden Fleece; very fine.
215 —— Half-doubloon (4 Scudi), same type, 1820; equally fine.
216 —— Dollar, sixteenth-doubloon; same type.
217 —— Twenty Pesetas of Barcelona, 4 dollars, or quarter-doubloon, 1813; very fine.
218 —— ISABELLA II. Piece of 80 reals, quarter-doubloon of 1839; very fine.
219 —— Piece of 100 reals ($5.00), 1850.
220 —— Same of 1862 (100 reals); very fine.
221 —— Piece of 10 escudos, 100 reals, or 5 dollars, of 1868; uncir., rare.
222 —— Four escudos, or 2 dolls.; same date, uncir.
223 —— Same of 2 do (1 dollar), and one of 20 reals; same value. 2 pieces

COINS OF PORTUGAL AND BRAZIL.

224 PETER II. 4000 Reis, A.D. 1700; a gold coin, arms of Portugal; rev. cross. Value in gold $5.00; rare.
225 JOSEPH I. 400 Reis (half-dollar) of 1763.
226 PIECE of 960 Reis (doll.) of 1819, and one without date: uncirculated. 2 pieces
227 Same of 1814, and 2000 do (new denomination) of Petrus II. (Dom Pedro), 1851 and 1869; value $1.00 each. 3 pieces
228 1000 Reis (half-doll.) of 1856 and 1859; uncirculated. 2 pieces
229 MISCELLANEOUS Spanish, Portuguese, and Brazilian Coins. 8 Macutas (African Colony); old pistareen of Philip II., restamped "200 reis;" quarter-dollar of Joseph Napoleon, etc., etc. Avoirdupois weight, 2 oz.

14   *Copper Coins of Spain.*

230 MISCELLANEOUS. Similar mis.; silver. 2 oz.
231 —— Similar to last. 2 oz.
232 —— Another lot. 2 oz.
233 —— Spanish and Mexican Silver (fine). 2 oz.
234 —— Same, with a mixture of S. American. 2 oz.
235 COB MONEY in the earliest and rudest form, with uncirculated pieces "Caracas." An *extremely fine selection.* 2 oz.
236 Another lot. 1½ oz.
237 EARLY Spanish pennies, groats, etc., base.   10 pieces

COPPER COINS OF SPAIN.
Ending with a few Portuguese and Brazilian Coppers.

238 HENRY I. (to 1214). Billon coins ENRICVS, etc., Lion; rev. Castle. And other old coins, unclassified; rare.
10 pieces

238* ALFONZO 10TH (1252). Two billon coins, with his bust crowned; rev. cross and castle. Fine and very rare, and others equally fine and old, unclassified. 10 pcs

239 HENRY II. (to 1368). Billon groat, bust, full face; rev. arms on shield of 4 semicircles; one monogram crowned, on lion and castle, with 5 others unclassified; valuable lot.   10 pieces

240 JOHN I. (1379.) Three billon coins; double J crowned, Agnus Dei and other types, with other old copper and billon coins; rare.   10 pieces

241 HENRY III. (1390.) Billon coins and others; extremely fine lot.   10 pieces

242 HENRY IIII. (1454.) Fine and rare billon coins, groat size; bust, full face, and others.   10 pieces

243 FERDINAND AND ISABELLA (to 1516). Six fine coppers, and with these, 4 others.   10 pieces

244 PHILIP I., II., III., and IV. (to 1621). All remarkably fine.   15 pieces

245 CHARLES II. to Philip V. 1665–1746. Chiefly restamped, "Corba" and "Cob money." A rare and interesting lot.   16 pieces

246 UNCLASSIFIED coins, selected for rarity of type and good preservation; all old.   15 pieces

247 ANOTHER selection, including fine coppers struck for Spanish Guiana.   15 pieces

248 FINE uncirculated coins of Catalonia, and good pieces of Barcelona, etc., one with the Maltese cross on rev.; rare.   10 pieces

Spanish Medals.

10   249 MEDALS and Medalets, Acclamation pieces, etc., etc. Proof coins of fine workmanship, local medals commemorative of important events, etc.; seldom equalled for quality. Heads of Chas. IV., Ferd. VII., and Isabella. *Valuable.*   15 pieces

12   250 As nearly a repetition of last as can be made; very fine, but not equal to the first.   15 pieces

13   251 CHARLES I. and Joanna, and other old coins. Several with the Jerusalem cross (square in the centre), with many rare and well preserved.   20 pieces

11   252 Quite similar to last.   20 "
11   253 Another selection.   20 "
10   254 Repetition of last.   20 "
11   255 The same.   20 "
11   256 Similar lot.   20 "
11   257 Another.   20 "
7   258 PORTUGUESE and Brazilian Coins.   15 "

SPANISH MEDALS.

Lead.

12   259 PHILIP II., Charles III., and Charles IIII., and other old medals of large size, with battered edges.   6 pieces

11   260 CHARLES IV. and Queen Eliza, Ferdinand VII., and others. Fine medals.   6 pieces

11   261 VELARDE Dadiz, Madrid, 1839 (one side only), and ALA LEALTAD SACRIFCADO 2 DO MAY, 1808 (one side); with fine medals of Isabella II., "War of Aflıca," French Exhibition, etc.   6 pieces

11   262 MEDALS with 3 heads, purposely defaced. MEDIZAGAL. CALATRAVA ARGVELLES de Febrero, 1857. Size 22.   2 pieces

Bronze.

9   263 FOR glorious deeds at Vera Cruz, 30 Oct. 1810. Ferd. VII., and other old medals of little importance.   4 pieces

15   264 CHAS. III.; rev. monument, OVI - INGENVAS, etc., silver-plated, size 42, with a marriage medal of his son, afterwards Chas. IV.; busts of the Prince and Pincess; well preserved.   2 pieces

7/5   265 CHAS. III. and Chas. IV. and wife; rev. visit to a gold mine, 1785, fine, size 40; and one of Charles IV. and Queen Eliza, 1796, (size 38), ex. fine.   2 pieces

16 *Coins of Mexico, Central and South America.*

266 "La Triple Garantia" Ferd. VII., "SUBACTA PERFIDEÆ, etc." "RESTAURADORA, DE LA EUROPA, un Americana Amigo," etc. All American medals. Extra fine and rare; in the same order as described, size, 32, 34, 34.   3 pieces

267 Old Medals of Charles III. and IIII., 2 silver-plated. Size, 32 and 30.   5 pieces

268 Charles III. Bust; rev. Hispania seated, attendants standing in the midst of a prosperous agricultural region. "Coloniac Gemellae, ad. Marianos Moules et Bacticani," 1784. Extra fine; size, 36.

269 Silver-Plated Medals of Charles III., IIII., and Ferd. VII.   3 pieces

270 Fine Gilt Medals of Charles IV. *by Gil*, of his series of 1790. Size, 28.   2 pieces

271 Others; no duplicates, splendid. Size, 25.   4 pieces

272 Ferdinand VII. Gilt Medals relating to Mexico. Two oval.   3 pieces

273 —— Silver-plated medal and two others. Size, 28. 3 pieces

274 Isabella. Bust (*by Pingret*); rev., "In memoria de los Hechos Heroicos." (Size, 36). "Salustiana de Olozaga," *by Estruck*, (size, 28), and two oval Caban water-works medal.   4 pieces

275 Mint Medals of Seville, 1856, two varieties, and Cuban Medal of 1867. Fine proof. Size, 28.   3 pieces

COINS OF MEXICO, CENTRAL AND SOUTH AMERICA.

276 Mexico. Real of Genl. Morelas, struck in copper; obv. bow and arrow, SUD.; rev. Mo. IR., 1812; rare.

277 —— Prov. of Zacatecas, Quartilla, brass; obelisk, decorated with garlands; rev. Cherub with Liberty cap in rays; half of same. Rare and ex. fine.   2 pieces

278 —— Others of Zacatecas Ialasco San Louis Potosi, Iuanajuato, etc. Rare lot of copper coins.   10 pieces

279 —— Ordinary lot coppers.   10 pieces

280 —— Augustus I. (Iturbide), *Onza De Oro*. Doubloon, 1822, bare bust; rev. imperial eagle on a cactus, decorated with Indian arms. Uncirculated, very rare.

281 —— *Onza De Oro*. Doubloon of the next year, equally fine and rare, and a different type, the arms on a shield.

282 —— ½ *Onza De Oro*, half Doubloon, same as last. Uncirculateder, very rare.

283 —— Another half Doubloon, same as last, equally fine.

284 —— Dollar (8 Reals) of Augustus I., 1822. Uncirculated, rare.

Coins of Mexico, Central and South America.

/0 0	285	MEXICO. Duplicate Dollar, nearly as fine.
2¢	286	—— Quarter, eighth, and sixteenth, same, fine. 3 pieces
20	287	—— Quarters. Ordinary. 3 pieces
/0 5	288	—— Old Republic. Gold 1-16 (Dollar), 1833, very fine.
2/0	289	—— ⅛ Onza (two Dollars), red gold and yellow gold, very fine, 1849. 2 pieces
17.37	290	—— Doblon or Doubloon of 1868. *Onza de Oro.* Weight, 417 - 707 grains troy. Value, 15.61, gold. Extremely fine, nearly proof.
21.35	291	—— TWENTY PESOS (20 Dollars) of gold of the present Republic, 1873. Uncirculated and brilliant.
/.25	292	—— Emperor Maximilian. Uncirculated Dollar, 1866.
/90	293	—— Dollar, half do., ten and five Cents. 165 cts. int. value; the lot.
?	294	—— Dollar, two Dimes, and half do. (125 cts.); the lot.
65	295	—— Imperial copper Centavo, 1864; *very rare*, fine.
55	296	—— Duplicate; equally fine, rare.
55	297	—— Dollar, half, and quarter of the new Republic, 1870 ? fine. 3 pieces
9¢	298	—— Same (Dollar), with Chinese marks.
1.05	299	—— Dollar of 1873, the old type. Uncirculated, rare.
/0	300	—— Quarter Reals. Uncirculated. 3 pieces
8.75	301	CENTRAL AMERICA. Republic of 1850, ½ *Onza de Oro*, half Doubloon of Costa Rica. Extremely fine.
3.90	302	—— Two Escudos (4 Dolls.) of same, gold.
95	303	—— Half Escudos (1 Doll.) of same, gold.
25	304	—— Quarter Dollars of the Republic, del Ecuador, 1831. Ordinary. 2 pieces
/5	305	—— Small Silver Coins of the various Republics of Central America. (Int. value, 50 cts.) 7 pieces
56	306	—— Guatemala, by General Carrera; obv. bust of the Gen.; rev. arms of Guatemala; un Peso, half do, eighth do; very fine, rare. 3 pieces
35	307	—— Guatemala Proclamation for Iturbide, eighth-doll., 1822; Proclamation 21 Mar., 1847, same denomination, one quarter-doll. size; "Iuiceo Por Juradas," *EL Puebla*, and half-dolls. of Carrera (one pierced) and Costa Rica. (Int. value $1.50.) 5 pieces
16 80	308	SOUTH AMERICAN Republic of New Granada, *Onza De Oro.* Doubloon of 1840; obv. head of Liberty; rev. arms of New Granada, DIEZ. I - SEIS - PESOS. BOGOTA -S. Uncirculated, very rare.
16 25	309	—— Another doubloon of New Granada, same type, but struck *at Popayan*, 1846; still more rare.

2

18 *Coins of Mexico, Central and South America.*

<small>1." " </small> 310 SOUTH AMERICAN Republic of New Granada. Piece of 10 dolls. value (gold), 1855 ; very fine and rare.

<small>1.0 5</small> 311 —— Silver dollars of New Granada, of different types; all from the mint of Bogota. VALE OCHO REALES = un PESO = LEI OCHO DINEROS = and DIEZ REALES, 1847, 1839, and 1858. All uncommon in this fine condition.   4 pieces

<small>/ o o</small> 312 —— Another lot of dollars from same mint; only two varieties.   5 pieces

<small>1 22</small> 313 —— A good lot of quarter-dolls. (VALE Dos REALES) from the mints of Bogota and *Popayan*. (Rare.)   5 pieces

<small>11</small> 314 —— Reals, half-real, and quarter do, Bogota ; fine and rare lot, uncirculated.   4 pieces

<small>8.75</small> 315 —— ECUADOR ½ *Onza De Oro*, half-doubloon, 1838 (4 escudos, $8.00). Very fine.

<small>2 /</small> 316 —— Quarters (2 reals) of Ecuador; various types and dates.   5 pieces

<small>45</small> 317 —— Republic of Venezuela, 2 half-dolls. and 1 quarter.

<small>11</small> 318 —— Copper coins of Venezuela, 2 centavos (varieties), half and quarter do ; uncirculated.   4 pieces

<small>/ 2</small> 319 —— Republic of Colombia, base dollars of 1820 and '21, and a variety of quarters (4 pieces); in all   6 pieces

<small>4.25</small> 320 —— Gold quarter-ounce (or quarter-doubloon) from the mint of *Quito*, in Colombia, 1835.

<small>10.62</small> 321 —— Diez Pesos (10 dollars), gold (900–1000 fine), from the mint of *Popayan*, in the United States of Colombia, 1866 ; extra fine, very rare.

<small>75</small> 322 —— Gold dollar, pierced ; Bogota.

<small>40</small> 323 —— Carthagena copper coin. Indian seated under a tree, at his back, cabin. Very rare, rude work.

<small>17.50</small> 324 —— Republic of Peru, *Onza De Oro*, doubloon (8 escudos, 16 dolls.), from the mint of *Lima*, 1863. Fine.

<small>1.70</small> 325 —— Eighth-doubloon, or $2.00, of 1828. Poor.

<small>1.00</small> 326 —— Uncirculated dollars of North and South Peru (Lima and Cuzco); scarce.   2 pieces

<small>40</small> 327 —— Half and quarter-dollars of Lima and Cuzco. Two of each ; fine.   4 pieces

<small>. 45</small> 328 —— Dollar, half, quarter, eighth, and sixteenth of same ; *desirable set*.   5 pieces

<small>37</small> 329 —— Duplicate set (quarter pierced).   5 "

<small>2.55</small> 330 —— Republic of Boliviana, *Onza De Oro* (doubloon) with bust of Bolivar in military dress, 1839; very fine and rare.

Coins of Mexico, Central and South America. 19

70   331   SOUTH AMERICA. Dollar of Boliviana; pierced.
110   332   —— Fine dollars of Boliviana, naked bust and mailed bust, 1835–1850; rev. a lama lying down on each side of a palm-tree, 6 stars and 9 stars above the tree.   Rare.   2 pieces
105   333   —— Dollars, with bust and without; 1 pierced.   2   "
50   334   —— Half-dollar and quarter do; ex. fine.   2   "
"   335   —— Half-dollars; fine.   2   "
17,90   336   —— *La Plata*, or Argentine Confederacy, doubloon of 1835; obv. head of the Sun, PROVINCIAS DEL RIO DE LA PLATA; rev. arms of the Confederacy, EN UNION Y LIBERTAD. Brilliant uncirculated coin; very rare.
110   337   —— Silver dollars, same type; 1 very fine.   2 pieces
25   338   —— Quarters, various types.   5   "
2.35   339   —— Dollar of Rioja (same Confederacy); obv. a mountain rising from the sea, in the foreground trophies displayed, 1838; rev. arms, ETERNO LOOR AL RETAVR-ADOR ROSAS. Uncirculated, very rare.
1.50   340   —— Dollar of the Province of Cordoba (same Confederacy); obv. Sun in double effulgence; rev. a castle flying a flag, with flags to r. and l. displayed, 1852. Very fine, rare.
65   341   —— Half-dollar of Cordoba; equally fine and rare.
45   342   —— Half-dollars to match 339 and 340; poor.   2 pieces
17.85   342*   —— Republic of Chili, *Onza De Oro*, doubloon of 1818 (8 escudos, 16 dolls.); extremely fine, rare.
8.00   343   —— Half-doubloon; same date, pierced.
17.85   344   —— Doubloon of 1839 (Chili); very fine, rare.
8.05   345   —— Half-doubloon (Chili). IGVALDAD ANTE LA LEI, 4 E(scudos), 1837, hand on a vol. ins. " Constitution;" rev. arms supported by a crowned lama and condor.
10.75   346   —— 10 pesos (10 dolls.), 1853, Liberty standing; rev. arms as before. Gold; very fine and rare.
1.50   347   —— Two dolls. and doll.; gold.   2 pieces
100   348   —— Chili. Dollar of Santiago, "UN PESO;" obv. volcano, column, globe, and star, 1821; fine, scarce.
95   349   —— UN PESO, 1869. Condor to l.; very fine.
125   350   —— Same. Condor to r.; very fine dollar.
60   351   —— Dollar, half, and quarter; fine.   3 pieces
55   352   —— Repetition of last.   3   "

1/   353   COPPER coins of Brazil and Portugal; large and small.
                 10 pieces

20   *Coins of France.*

354 SPANISH, Portuguese, and Brazilian.   10 pieces
355 Another lot.   10   "
356 AFRICAN, copper, two macutas, gilt medal of Dom Pedro, young head, old pennies of Spain, etc., etc.   10 pieces
357 HAYTI. Base dollar, half, quarter, and eighth of Pres. Boyer; fine (1 pierced).   4 pieces
358 —— Half, quarters (2); 1 pierced.   3 pieces
359 —— Faustin I. 1 Pres. Geffrard, etc. Nearly all uncirculated; copper.   4 pieces
360 JAVA Sumatra and E. Indies coppers.   5 pieces
361 CHINESE Cash.   28 pieces
362 MOORISH COINS, with two triangles linked; in the centre a large pellet or ball; on the reverse, the date in Arabic figures, as 1252, 1258, 1260, 1262, 1268, 1272. Some have no date, but the double triangle on *both* sides. Others have Arabic letters as well as figures. Probably struck for circulation in some FRENCH Colony in Africa. We have called them "Moorish" Coins without any certain knowledge, or authority for so doing. We are constantly meeting with stray examples of these coins, but this is the first *collection* of them with varieties that we have seen. Exceptionally fine and interesting lot.   20 pieces

COINS OF FRANCE.
Gold.

363 LOUIS XVIII., 20 Francs, 1814; fine.
364 CHARLES X., 20 Francs, 1830; fine.
365 REPUBLIC, 20 Francs, 1849; fine.
366 NAPOLEON III., 20 Francs, 1857; fine.
367 NAPOLEON III., 20 Francs, 1863; fine.
368 NAPOLEON III., 20 Francs, 1867, *by Barre*.   Uncirculated.
369 NAPOLEON III., 10 Francs, 1865,   "   "
370 NAPOLEON III., 5 Francs,   "   Proof.
371 NAPOLEON III., 5 Francs,   "   Ordinary.

Silver.

372 PENNY OF THE CRUSADES (JOHN ?) and various old groats.
                                                            7 pieces
373 LOUIS XIV., 1713. Eighth Crowns.   2 pieces
374 LOUIS XV., fine Crown, 1720; rare.
375 —— Jetons (¼ Crowns); beautiful.   2 pieces
376 —— Same and quarter Crown; poor.   2 pieces

United States Coins. 21

1.00 377 Louis XVI. Crown, 1794 ; fair.
1.00 378 —— Same, 1795; rev. REGNE DE LA LOI; in ex. L'AN 5 DE LA LIBERTE. Nearly uncirculated, rare.
27 379 —— Quarter Crown ; very good.
92 380 Republia Five Francs L'An., 11 ; fair.
92 381 Napoleon I. Five Francs, 1808-11-12.   3 pieces
70 382 —— Francs and two do. (4 Francs).   3 pieces
95 383 Louis XVIII. Five Francs, 1820 ; fine.
95 384 Charles X. Same 1830; fine.
20 385 Louis Philippe. 1 Franc, 1847; very fine.
20 386 Republic. One Franc, 1849 ; very fine.
92 387 Napoleon III. Five Francs, 1856-1869; fair.   2 pieces
25 388 —— Two and one do. very fine.   2 pieces
90 389 —— Medal of the Expedition of Mexico ; fine and rare.
1.60 390 Present Republic and other Coins, 8½ Francs ; the lot.
per the lot.

Copper.

5 391 Jetons of Louis XIV., and later with representations of the "Holy Gate." A picked lot, with a number of miscellaneous Coins.   24 pieces
5 392 Miscellaneous Copper Coins (all of France).   10 pieces
3 393 Same.   10 pieces
3 394 Same.   10 pieces
3 395 Same.   10 pieces
3 396 Same.   20 pieces
2 397 Same, not classified.   15 pieces
10 398 Same, French and English, *Canadian*.   15 pieces
10 399 Same, Canadian.   10 pieces

UNITED STATES COINS.

Gold.

21.75 400 Double Eagle, 1864, ($20); fine.
21.75 401 Double Eagle, 1873, ($20); fine
5.40 402 Half Eagle, 1861, ($5); "
3.30 403 Three Dolls, 1856, ($3); "
2.75 404 Quarter Eagle, 1852, ($2½); "
1.05 405 Dollar, 1869, ($1); bruised.

Silver.

5 5   406 PINE TREE SHILLING (old counterfeit), good condition.
1 0 6   407 EBLING'S COLUMBIAN GARDEN, 200 BOWERY, N. Y. Stamped on a Spanish Quarter Dollar.
6 6   408 YOUNG, THE MAGICIAN, stamped on a Spanish Quarter Dollar.
1 0 0   409. DOLLAR of 1860.
1 0 5 −   410 DOLLAR of 1874.
5 0   411 HALF-DOLLARS of 1805-7-29-32-34-61 and '73.   7 pieces
25−   412 QUARTER-DOLLS. of 1805-6-21-37-53-57-58-61 and '73. 10 pcs
1 6 0   413 DIME of 1805; very fine.
1 1 0   414 DIMES of different dates, taken from circulation, and generally pierced.   8 pieces
1 0   415 DIMES, uncirculated, 1854-71-72-73 and '74.   6 pieces
5−   416 HALF-DIMES. Pierced.   6 pieces
5−   417 HALF-DIMES, uncirculated, 1830-32-35-50 and '72, and two nickels.   10 pieces
4   418 THREE CENTS.   6 pieces
70   419 BADGE or Medalet, with loop. Struck by a Secret (?) Society in New Orleans. 1858. SOCIEDAD YBERA DE BENEF^a. MVTVA ANO, 1858., N. O. Two flags crossed. Size, 16; rare.

Copper.

3 0   420 LOUISIANA CENT; 1767, poor.
1 7   421 ONE DIME, 1861. Struck in copper, and probably *not* at the United States Mint. A curiosity.
1 ½   422 A LOT OF CENTS and Copperheads of no value.   53 pieces

---

MISCELLANEOUS SILVER COINS.

35−   423 BRACTEATE, Ecclesiastical pieces; old thin coins of German cities, etc., selected from thousands; all fine and uncommon, a majority of them of the Quarter Dollar size, but thinner.   10 pieces
3 2   424 MALTESE (De-Rohan), old Spanish (Henry 4th), German, 1544, etc., etc., about the size of last.   10 pieces
3 2   425 Similar lot.   10 pieces
15   426 BRILLIANT uncirculated Coins of the 18th and present centuries, average Quarter Doll. size, German, of varying intrinsic value. Beautiful.   10 pieces
12   427 Similar lot, very fine, German, French, and Spanish. Same size.   10 pieces

Coins of England.

12	428 Similar, all uncirculated, average Dime size.	10 pieces
10	429 Another lot like last, uncirculated, but base.	10 pieces
6	430 Similar, but smaller, beautiful.	20 pieces
8¢	431 FIVE FRANCS AND THALERS, Belgium, Prussia and Austria; poor.	10 pieces
65	432 Similar Thalers.	10 pieces
	433 OLD silver coins, avoirdupois weight; mostly German, and more or less base.	3 oz
	434 Similar lot.	3 oz
	435 Similar.	3 oz
	436 Similar.	3 oz
0	437 Similar.	3 oz
2	438 Similar.	3 oz
4	439 Similar.	3 oz
	440 Similar.	3 oz
	441 Similar.	3 oz
	442 Similar.	3 oz
	443 Similar.	3 oz
	444 Similar.	3 oz
5	445 BASE coins.	32 pieces
10	446 SWISS coins; base, uncirculated.	5 "
6	447 Similar; not as fine.	20 "
6	448 Similar.	15 "
4	449 SILVER coins, franc and half-franc; 2 of each.	4 "

COINS OF ENGLAND.

Gold.

5.25	450 GEORGE IV. Sovereign, 1826; fine.	
5.25	451 VICTORIA. Sovereign, 1862; fine.	
5.35	452 —— Rev. St. George, 1871; uncirculated, rare.	
5.25	453 —— Sovereign; rev. Australia, 1866.	
5.25	454 —— Same; rev. Australia, 1868.	
2.65	455 —— Half-sovereigns.	2 pieces

Kings of Northumberland.

1.00	456 ETHELRED, A.D. 840-849. Obv. † EDILRED REX, pellet in a beaded circle; rev. † EARDVLF, pellet in a circle as before. Ruding Pl. 10, No. 14; Well. No. 1932. R.R.; Styeæ; very fine.	

24   *Coins of England.*

Sole Monarchs.
[All silver.]

2/2   457 EDGAR. 959–975. Obv. † EADGAR REX, small cross in a circle; rev. † FATTOLF-MO, cross in circle as before; extremely fine broad penny (solidus), and according to Well. RRR, Ruding Pl. 21, No. 17. £3 sterling.

175   458 CANUTE I. (The Great) 1015–1035. Obv. † CNVT REX AN, head in helmet, to left, sceptre; rev. PILLE IREM TO EOFR (York), double cross, in the centre, rose; in the angles, a pellet. Compare with Ruding Pl. 23, No. 19; Well., No. 1940, RRR. As it fell from the die.

1.60   459 EDWARD the Confessor. 1042–1066. EAD PAR. DR REX, crowned bust to r., with sceptre; rev. cross; probably struck at York. Compare with Well. 1943 RR, and Ruding Pl. 24, No. 10. As fine as last.

Anglo-Norman.
Silver.

2,75   460 WILLIAM 1ST (The Conqueror). 1066–1087. Bust, full face, crown and sceptre, PILLELM REX; rev. cross within a circle, in the angles on rings, the letters P A X S. Beautiful, as it came from the die; rare.

50   461 HENRY II. 1154–1189. Extremely fine broad penny.

1,00 462 RICHARD I. (Cœur de Lion) 1189–1196. Denier (Poictiers); very fine, rare.

60   463 EDWARD I. 1272–1307. Penny, EDWRA, etc.; very fine.

100   464 EDWARD II. 1307–1327. Penny, EDWAR, etc.; fair.

1,50 465 EDWARD III. 1327–1377. Groat, London. Uncirculated, very broad; rare.

50   466 —— Groat and half-groat, London; very fine. 2 pieces

1,25 467 EDWARD, The Black Prince. 1376. Half-groat. The Prince seated to r. with drawn sword; rev. long cross and double circle of inscription; well preserved. RRR.

[This is given with strong doubts as to the correctness of the attribution. It *may* be right, and at all events is a very rare and remarkable *English* coin.]

1,75 468 RICHARD II. 1377–1399. Full face, crowned head on a rose, RICARD; rev. CIVITAS, LONDON, etc. As it was coined; groat. R.

100   469 HENRY V. 1413–1422. Extremely fine groat, struck at Calais; scarce.

Coins of England. 25

15   470   HENRY VI. 1422–1471. Extra fine London Groat; rare.
4/5   471   HENRY VIII. 1509–1547. Groat and half-groat. HEN-RICVS VIII. crowned, profile, bust; fine.   2 pieces
5.00   472   EDWARD VI. 1547–1553. Crown of 1551 (the first coined in England). One of the best that have come to us, but little the worse for circulation; very rare.
3 c   473   MARY. 1553–1558. Groat and sixpence of Philip and Mary; poor.   2 pieces
3 c   474   ELIZABETH. 1558–1603. Shilling, without date, and half-shilling, 1567; broad and fine.   2 pieces
50   475   JAMES I. 1603–1625. Shilling and half-shilling; fine (the first unusually so).   2 pieces
9 c   476   CHARLES I. 1625–1649. Half-crown, below the horse EBOR; fine and *very rare*.
50   477   —— Shilling, rare type, and about as it came from the dies; very broad, desirable.
3 o   478   —— 4d, 3d, 2d, and farthings, and penny of the Commonwealth; fine.   7 pieces
1.00   479   COMMONWEATH. 1649–1658. Shilling, 1653, nearly uncirculated; rare.
5,25   480   CROMWELL, to 1658. Half crown, bust to l.; rev. shield crowned, PAX. QVAERITVR BELLO; hardly circulated, very fine and rare.
6,00   481   —— Shilling; *uncirculated*, rare.
8,10   482   —— Oval medal, bust of Cromwell, WORD AT DVNBAR, THE LORD OF HOSTS, etc. Head side only, uncirculated impression, copper-plated, 13 x 16. See Well. 2024; compare with Van Loon II-356. Very rare.
1,40   483   CHARLES II. 1661–1685. Coronation Medal by *Simon*, 1661, bust crowned; rev. EVERSO MISSVS, an angel crowning the King - VAN LOON II. 470; extremely fine, rare.   Size 19
1,75   484   —— Crown, 1673, laureated bust in Roman habit; extremely fine, but little circulated.
85   485   —— Half crown, same type; fair, rare.
37   486   —— Shilling, same type; fine.
1 c   487   —— Sixpence, groat, half-groat, and penny; uncirculated, very rare.   4 pieces
75   488   JAMES II. 1685–1689. Half-Crown, 1687. Uncirculated, rare.
2 c   489   —— Groat, Half-Groat, and Penny. Uncirculated. 3 pieces
6 5   490   WILLIAM AND MARY. 1689–1695. Half-Crown, 1689. Uncirculated, rare.
12   491   —— Twopence and Penny. Uncirculated.   2 pieces

Coins of England.

6|5   492 WILLIAM III. (alone). Half-Crown, 1698. Uncirculated, very rare.
3 0   493 —— Shilling. Uncirculated, very rare.
5 3   494 —— Set Maundy Money, 4d., 3d., 2d., 1d.; fair.
1 6 0   495 ANNA. 1702–1714. Crown; Plumes and roses, 1701; fine, scarce.
5 0   496 —— Shilling, 1711. Uncirculated; very rare.
2 0   497 —— Sixpence. Uncirculated; very rare.
7 c   498 —— Groat. Uncirculated, brilliant; very rare.
1 0   499 —— Threepence and Penny; fair.   2 pieces
2–7   500 GEORGE I. 1714–1727. Shilling and Sixpence, South Sea Co's. issue; very fine.   2 pieces
15   501 —— Twopence and Penny; fair.   2 pieces
25   502 GEORGE II. 1727–1760. Shilling; roses, brilliant; rare.
12   503 —— Sixpence, brilliant; rare.
40   504 —— Set Maundy Money, 4d., 3d., 2d., 1d. Uncirculated, rare.
2 6   505 —— Shilling; poor.
17   506 GEORGE III. 1760–1820. Shilling and Sixpence (1787). Brilliant.   2 pieces
25   507 —— Shilling, 1817; rev. arms within the Collar of the Order of the Garter; brilliant, rare.
7   508 —— 4d., 2d., and Penny. Uncirculated.   3 pieces
1,70   509 —— Bank Tokens, Colonials, etc., 8s. sterling the lot.
25   510 —— The Peterboroug Bank Token for 18 pence, with view of the Cathedral. Northumberland and Durham Token for 1s., and Fizeley Shilling Token, all brilliant. 3 pcs
4 2   511 GEORGE IV. 1820–1830. Half-Crown and Shilling. 2 pieces
50   512 —— Proof set of Maundy Money; rare.
2 7   513 WILLIAM III. 1830–1837. Shilling and Sixpence. Uncirculated.   2 pieces
6 0   514 —— Other Coins, 3s. sterling; the lot.
1,5¢   515 VICTORIA Crowned in 1837. Her Pattern Gothic Crown. A proof impression, tarnished, but extremely fine and rare.
1 25   516 —— Her Crown of 1845, also very scarce, very fine.
5 0   517 —— Florins of 1852 and '3, brilliant.   2 pieces
15   518 —— Shilling and Sixpence, brilliant.   2 pieces
1,10 Lot   519 —— Shilling, 20 cents, Florins and East India Coins. Intrinsic value, 5s. ($1.00). uncirculated; the lot.
1.13 Lot   520 —— Rupee, and small Coins. Intrinsic value, 7f. ($1.14); the lot.

SILVER COINS OF SCOTLAND.

521 ALEXANDER III. 1249-1286. Penny; bust in profile with sceptre; rev. cross, mullets with angels; fine.

522 DAVID II. 1329-1371. Half-Groat, side-face crowned with sceptre erect, the outline of a rose around the head, all within a beaded circle; rev. DNS PROTECTOR MS & LIBERATOR MS-VILLA EDINBVRGH, in two circles divided by a cross, with stars in the angles; ex. fine, rare.

523 ROBERT II. 1371-1390. Side-face Groat, similar to last; very fine.

524 ROBERT III. 1390-1406. Groat, full-face, with crown, no sceptre, all on a rose; rev. similar to last, but with balls instead of stars; very fine and rare.

525 JAMES V. Fine Billon Coin; rev. star of five points in the centre of a cross, a small cross and crown in each angle.

526 JAMES V. 1513-1542. Groat, side-face, closed crown, JACOBVS 5, etc.; rev. OPPIDVM EDINBVRGI; extremely fine, rare.

527 MARY. 1542-1587. Shilling, 1558. Arms on a shield, crowned; rev. large and small crosses; very fine.

528 —— Billon Coin, with similar of her son (James VI.), and others. 6 pieces

ENGLISH COPPER COINS AND MEDALS.

529 "A BRISTOL Farthing," 1662; very rare.

530 "GREAT Yarmouth, for the Use of the Poor," 1669; brass farthing, very rare.

531 "A COVENTRY half penny, 1669."

532 "THIS farthing is owned in Tetbury, 1669."

533 "A GLOUCESTER farthing, 1669."

534 "A STAMFORD half-penny," etc.

535 CAROLUS A Carolo farthing, 1675; *uncirculated*.

536 JAMES II. "Gun money" and "Hibernia;" fine. 4 pieces

537 WILLIAM and Mary and William III. Half-pennies and farthings. 3 pieces

538 ANNA Farthing, 1714; uncirculated, very rare.

539 GEORGE I. Half-penny (very fine) and farthing; uncirculated. 2 pieces

540 GEORGE II. Half-penny (very fine) and farthing; uncirculated. 2 pieces

541 GEORGE III. Two-penny, bright, uncirculated; r c.
542 —— Penny, half do, two farthings; varieties, uncirculated.
4 pieces
543 —— Ceylon Elephant penny, 1812; proof.
544 GEORGE IV. Penny, half do, and two farthings; varieties, bright and uncirculated. 4 pieces
545 WILLIAM IV. Penny, quarter-Anna, and two farthings; uncirculated. 4 pieces
546 VICTORIA. Pennies, and smaller; uncirculated. 10 "
547 —— Canadian and various. 10 "
548 MEDAL of Mary I. Of her time, head side only; large lead medal; Pitt medal in brass; old Fireman's medal, Anti-slavery, and Vernon. 5 pieces
549 —— MARY II. 1694 (Born and died). Fine bronze. Size 32
550 —— ANNA. Vigo, Born 1802; Sardinia, etc., 1808; splendid medals, bronze. Size 24. 3 pieces
551 —— GEORGE III. Rev. Fides Militum, 1715; fine proof, bronze. By *Croker*. Size 28
552 —— Rev. "Junguntur opes Firmatur imperium," 1st Jan., 1801; bronze. Size 32
553 —— George IV. on his coronation, and one of Queen Caroline; very fine, bronze. 26 and 32. 2 pieces
554 —— "The Young Roscius," and "Princess Charlotte"; fine bronze. Size 24. 2 pieces
555 —— Martin Folkes, 1743, bust; rev. pyramid; fine proof, rare; one of Earl St. Vincent, Earl Howe, and Samuel Johnson. 4 pieces
556 —— Declaration of the Congress of Vienna, 1815. "To arms;" bronze, proof. Size 26
557 —— "The English army on the Tagus," 1810; bronze.
Size 28
558 —— Victoria on her Coronation, her picture to the waist, by *Ottley;* bronze, proof, very rare. Size 32
559 —— The *Birmingham* series of Exposition medals, struck in tin. They bear heads of the Prince Consort and Queen, sometimes together, sometimes single, and view of the Crystal Palace; strictly fine proofs. Size 24 and 32. (4 of each.) 8 pieces
560 —— Other tin medals by *Ottley*, same subject as last; splendid proof. Size 46. 2 pieces
561 —— Others, one on same subject; Thames Tunnel, with head of Brunel, and Anti-Corn-Law medal; all fine proofs. Size 28. 3 pieces
562 —— Miscellaneous white Medals. 10 pieces

Old Hammered Silver Coins, Dollar Size.

1,10   563 EMPEROR Ferdinand I., Germany, 1565 (Tyrol); not rubbed, but stained; rare.
7,0c   564 JOHN GEORGE, Saxony, 1614. Mailed figure to the middle, drawn sword, head bare; rev. bust of Augustus, circumscribed by 18 coats-of-arms on shields; extremely fine.
2 0 c 565 —— Crown of 1620, coat-of-arms, *two* angels supporting; rev. coat-of-arms, one angel supporting; fine and rare.
2 7s   566 FERDINAND II., Austria. Crown of 1624, the King standing, crowned, sceptre erect and globe; uncirculated.
2 7s   567 —— Same, as Emperor of Germany, the Emperor standing with shields and javelin; uncirculated, very rare.
16c   568 LEOPOLD, Arch Duke, Austria, 1624; superb crown, bust, head bare.
15 c   569 MAXIMILLIAN, Count Pal, Archduke, and Elector, Saxony, etc. Broad crown, Madonna and child; rev. arms of Saxony, etc., 1625.
2 c c 570 LUBEC crown of Ferd. II. 1626. Half-length figure of St. John the Baptist; uncir., rare.
2 7s   571 FERDINAND III., Emperor. Laureated bust, lace collar over the shoulders; rev. arms of Austria; fine crown of 1649.
5 25   572 MONASTERY of Westphalia. St. Paul in the air above the city, coat-of-arms, with 5 crests, quotation from 143d Psalm; extremely broad (size 31) crown, without date.
2 5c   573 BRUNSWICK and Lunenburg. Crown of 1665, wild man with uprooted pine tree; extremely fine. Size 29
3,50   574 SQUARE Klippe, full crown size of John George of Saxony, bust; rev. inscription, 1678; uncirculated. 26 x 26.
5,57   575 —— Another Klippe, 1669, cypher of his name (John George); rev. young Hercules in his cradle crushing serpents, ABINCVNABVLIS. Same size as last, and a finer piece; a full ounce in weight; very rare.
150   576 LEOPOLD I. Beautiful uncirculated crown, 1701.
20c   577 ARGENTORATENSIS. Rev. Lily; fine crown, without date.
250   578 SEDE Vacante crown of Fulda, 1788; uncirculated, rare.
2 2   579 AUGSBURG Confession, second Centennial, 1739, Lubec. The Church personified, walking with cross and open Bible; uncirculated and excessively rare.
30c   580 CROWN medal of Saxony; busts of the three brothers, Frederick, John George, and Johannes, with handsome ring frame, and loop; gilt.
15c   581 CROWN of George Louis (George 1st of England), Bruns. and Lun., St. Andrew, 1714; fine.

Milled Crowns.

2 oc 582 Pope Pius VI., 1780; broad milling; ex. fine.
1 00 583 Leopold III., Italy and Sicily, 1798; extremely fine.
1 50 584 Nuremberg dollar, 1765, view of the city; uncirculated.
1 oc 585 Leopold III. and Frederick II. Rev. (of last) shield surrounded by collar of the Order of the Garter; uncirculated, very rare. 2 pieces
1 60 586 Lubec. Dollar of 1752; uncirculated.
2 oo 587 Hamburg. Dollar of 1764; very fair, uncirculated.
1 c 5 588 Maria Theresa. "Ad Norman Convent," 1766; tin one of 1780; very fine. 2 pieces
1 oc 589 Maximilian Joseph, Bavaria. Uncirculated Crown of 1813, and same of 1819. 2 pieces
90 590 Francis I., Austria. Fine crown 1829.
1 05 591 Fred. Augustus, Saxony. X marks (crown) of 1776. Very fine.
1 10 592 Brunswick and Luneburg. Crown 1790. Uncirculated.. (1 species Thaler).
2 oc 593 Fred. VI., Denmark. Rigs-Daler. Crown of 1819. Nearly uncirculated.

Double Thalers, Thalers, etc.

1 50 594 Leopold Von Baden. Double thaler of 1852. Extra fine.
1 00 595 William II., Netherlands. 2½ Gulden (dollar) 1848. Extra fine.
1 50 596 William, King of Wurtemberg. 2 Gulden (80 cts.) 1846. Uncirculated.
"   597 Adolph, Nassau, 1846. 2 Gulden (80 cts.) Uncirculated.
9 c   598 Chas. Albert, Sardinia, 1837. 5 Lire (94 cts.) 1830—1837. Very fine. 2 pieces
80   599 Louis II., Hesse. 2 Gulden, 1846. Fine.
70   600 Fred. III., Prussia. Thalers. 3 pieces
6 5   601 Hanover, Saxony, Prussia, etc. Fine Thalers. Nearly uncirculated. 7 pieces
95   602 Ferd. IV., Sicily. Crown, 1805. and one of Ferd. I. (new Regime), 1818. Fair. 2 pieces
1 oc 603 One of Ferd. IV., 1805. Uncirculated; very rare.
1 50 604 Ferd. II. (120 grains). Crown of 1836. Fine.
"   605 Gregory XVI. Scudo (crown) of 1845, fine, and half scudo (50 Baiocchi). 2 pieces
6 5   606 Victor Emanuel. 5 Lire (1870), 2 Lire, 1 Lire, and 20 Centesimi. Uncirculated. 4 pieces

German Coins, etc., Continued. 31

1.35 607 RUSSIA. 25—20—10 Kopecs; others (Italian), all intrinsic value, 138 cts. All uncirculated. The lot.
.cr
10c 608 WILLIAM I., Schaumberg (extra thick coin), and William II., Ned., Rix Doll. and Gulden. Fine. 2 pieces
3.25 609 HESSIAN half dollar of the Landgrave Fred. II., for soldiers in the American war. Subsidy money received from England. Bust of the Landgrave; rev. shield on a star of 8 points, VIRTVTE ET FIDELITATE, 1776. "Ein Halber Thaler." Ex. fine and rare.

Old Hammered Coins of less than the Dollar Size.

6o   610 24 Marien Groschen, 1693. Hildescheim. Thaler value-
3c   611 20 G(roschen), Saxony. See No. 565, half of the crown there described; same type. Rare, with loops.
160 612 HALF crown of 1628, Salzburg. Two archbishops supporting a cathedral; rev. a procession of eccles. carrying relics. As fine as when struck. A very rare historical piece.
65   613 ⅔ crown of 1679. John Fred. Bruns; rev. "Ex Duris Gloria." Fine and rare.
1.50 614 ⅔ crown, 1702. City of Lunenburg. Fine.
105 615 24 Marien Groschen, 1738, Stolberg. (Thaler value). 2 pieces
30   616 —— Half same. Uncirculated. 3 pieces
75   617 ⅔ crown Leopold I., Germany, 1695, and others. Same value. Extremely fine and interesting lot. 6 pieces
45   618 Others with half and third dollars, 2 of each. Fine. 6 pieces
8c   619 SILVER MEDAL by Looz. Dir DEN BECHER DER FREU DEN LANGE NOCH SO WE HEUT! Fine work Size 23

Gold Coins.

1.10 620 HALF CROWN, without date. ($1.19).
10   621 BAPTISMAL Medalet, (gilt). Size 12
4.15 622 LEOPOLD II., Belgium. 20 Fr., 1870. Uncirculated.
4.30 623 WILLIAM, Netherlands, 10 G(ulden). Same as last, 1825.
4.15 624 FRANOIS JOSEPH, Hungary, 1872. 20 Fr. Rare.
5.25 625 LOUIS II., Baden. 20 M., ($5.00). Uncirculated.
4.30 626 CHAS. ALBERT, Sard., 1840. 20 L(ire), ($4.00) Fine.
5.20 627 WILLIAM, Prussia, 1872. (20 M.), ($5.00). Uncirculated.
1.10 628 RAFAEL CARRERA, Guatemala. Peso, (Doll.) Fine.

Bronze Medals.

1,70   629 MASONIC. "L'UNION DE FAMILE OR DE PARIS, 5786;" on one side the pillars, J(achin) and B(oas), fronting a temple with seven pillars; rev. emblems—octagon. Very fine.   Size 20

35   630 LOUIS XIV., *by Mauger*. Fine proofs. No duplicates. Size 26.   6 pieces

10   631 GALERIE Metallique. Visconte, Montgolfier, Chas. L'Brun, Edelinck, Destouches, Varin, Dexiles, Gerbier, Vaucanson, and Mezeray. In fine condition.   10 pieces

14   632 SERIES Numismatica. Cartesius, Boerhauve, Klopstock, Oxenstiern, Gellertus, Comarota, Gessner.   7 pieces

15   633 MISCELLANEOUS. John Locke, Vandyck, P. P. Rubens, and Richard. Valuable lot.   4 pieces

7   634 BRONZE and tin.   12 pieces

Miscellaneous.
Copper.

3   635 BAG containing 244 pieces.

5-2   636 SELECTED Lot. *Extra fine*.   50 pieces

6   637 ARABIAN Coins, ancient and modern.   48 pieces

Silver.

45   638 COINS of Ancient Spain (from the twelfth century), with Arabian legends. The form and size are similar to the old English pennies and groats, most of them being of the groat size. As fine as when struck.   6 pieces

3 c   639 Another lot, all groat size. Nearly as fine.   6 pieces

25   640 Others, some pierced. One old coin of Ferd. and Isabella. A more common lot.   10 pieces

[I find in the *Encyclopedie-Roret*, Paris, some of these coins figured, with the following descriptions:
"CASTILE, *Alphonse III.*, cette curieuse monnaie est un aufour du roi Alphonse, portant des legends arabes dont voici la traduction." | * Au centre en cinque lignes: "Le Prince | des Catholiques | Alphonse fils de sanche | que Dieu le Soutienne | par sou aide. Autour: *A ete frappé ci dinar à Toli te l'au 1255 de Safar*, (1217 de Jesus Christ);" rev. Au centro en trois lignas. "*L'imam de le Eglise chertienne, le pap de Rome ADF.*" Autour: "*Au nan du Pere du fils et du Saint-Esprit, Dieu est antique, celui qui voit et que est baptiste est sauve.*"
Others of similar fabric and style are Mohammedan, and on these we notice such little differences in the legend as this:
"*Mohammed est l'apotre de Dieu que l'a envoyé avec la direction et la religion veritable.*"]

40   641 LARGE and uncommonly fine piece of this money, and *square* Arab Coins. Two of each.   4 pieces

27   642 BRACTEATES, Turkish and Arab Silver Coins.   8 pieces

65   643 DOLLAR and half do., with Chinese punch or chop marks.   2 pieces

SILVER COINS OF THE ARSACIDAE AND SAS-SANIDAE.

1 40 644 ARSACES XXI. (Gotarces). Extremely fine drachma; head bearded and diademed; behind, large bow; rev. the king seated, holding a bow; in the field, letter A, ins. surrounding in straight double lines. R.

1 10 645 PHRAATES IV. Behind the head, eagle holding a crown in his beak, drachm; rare; compare with Well. No. 7075.

8 ¢ 646 Another. In the field, crescent and star. See Wellenheim, No. 7076; rare, 2.

7 5 647 ARSACES XXVIII. (Volosges, III.) Tetradrachm billon. Diademed head, heavy formal beard and hair; rev. figure standing to l., presenting a crown to the king, seated to r.; in very fine condition and extremely rare. Visconte, Pl. 7, No. 2.

1.10 648 ARTAXERXES OR ARDESHIR I. Didrachm; head with globe and diadem, long braided beard and hair; size, 18; rev. burning altar without attendants; legend in Pehlvic character. See Visconti, Pl. VIII., No. 1, did.; size, 18.

1 05 649 SAPOR I. Head with tiara and globe, short beard; rev. fire altar, and Magii standing; has loop. See Vis. P. VIII., No. 3; fine and rare didrachm; size, 18.

1 10 650 SAPOR II. Didrachms, same type, smaller; size, 16. 2 ps.

1 60 651 SAPOR III. Head surrounded by ins. and two beaded circles, Tiara with wings and plume, short beard; rev. lighted altar and magii; as it came from the die, superb; size, 21; very rare.

0 ¢ 652 VARARNES I. and II. Beardless head, same types as last. Beautiful examples, varieties; broad (size, 20). 3 pcs

ANCIENT GREEK COPPER COINS.

2 2 653 AFRICA (in general), Coins with representations of wild animals, elephant, lion, leopard, etc.; rude. 6 pcs

3 2 654 ATHENS. One rev. shield; one rev. tripod, etc. 3 pieces

2 5 655 BRUNDUSIUM. Head of Jupiter; rev. amphion on dolphin, BRVN; fine and rare, with coins of Carthage. Star within circle of pearls; rare lot. 5 pieces

1 2 656 BRUTTIUM and Acarnania. 4 pieces

2 4 657 CALENO; rev. Cock; fine and rare. 2 pieces

1 2 658 CORINTH; rev. Pegassus (very fine), and Locris. 4 pieces

,, 659 THURIUM AND SMYRNA; rev. polypus; rare. 3 pieces

34 Roman Republican Coins.

- *1 6* 660 PANORMUS and unknown. 8 pieces
- *12* 661 HIERO II., and others. 8 pieces
- *10* 662 ROMANCIA, GADES, etc. 8 pieces
- *12* 663 ARAB AND ROMANO-Spanish. 10 pieces
- *2 12* 664 JOTAPA (Queen of Commagene); head; rev. scorpion; a large broken coin, very rare. Romancia in Spain, two heads; Mytilene, head of Sappho, rev. lyre; fine and very rare. · One of Antiochus, Roman Imperial of Hadrian and others. Valuable lot. 8 pieces

GREEK SILVER.

- *1 30* 665 AGRIGENTUM, Eagle and Crab, didrachm; fine.
- *1 65* 666 CORINTH; rev. Pegassus; very fine didrachm.
- *1 00* 667 SELGE; rev. slinger; very fine didrachm.
- *1 90* 668 ATHENS; rev. owl, Tetradrachm; very good.
- *2,00* 669 LEONTIUM; rev. lion's head and 4 grains of barley; tet. fine, rare.
- *7 0* 670 CNYDUS. Lion's head, open mouth, drachm, fine, and one of Rhodes. 2 pieces
- *85* 671 DARIC and drachm of Phocis; both rare. 2 pieces
- *55* 672 TARENTUM; Chios; and Phoenician Coin; rev. TRIOS, prow; Did. and drachm. 3 pieces
- *45* 673 AEGINA and other small coins; oboli, hemidrachma and drachma. 6 pieces
- *6 5* 674 ARTAXERXES A.D. 226; obv. galley; rev. man facing a beast, both upright; hemidrachm; rare.

ROMAN REPUBLICAN, OR CONSULAR COINS—Silver.

- *2 C* 675 AEMILIA. Head of Juno, ROMA; rev. equestrian statue on a bridge, with arches, AEMILA; ex. fine, with one of Lepidus, same family, poor. 2 pieces
- *2 C* 676 ACILIA. Head casqued M.ACILIVS-MF; rev. Hercules in a quadriga, with others unclassified; good lot. 5 pieces
- *45* 677 AFRANIA. Obv. female head casqued; rev. Trinacrus, son of Neptune, standing one foot on a prow; rare to excess. See Wellenheim, 8,300 . RRRRR. Struck by *Allienus*, with others of the same family; all fine and rare. 5 pieces
- *75* 678 ANTONIA. A Coin of the VI. Legion, as fine as when struck, with others (one a quinarius). 4 pieces

Roman Republican Coins. 35

5 — 679 ANTONIA. Bare head of Marc Antony, M - ANT . IMP ; rev. temple of the sun, full-faced radiated head of Osiris ; another head of Venus, Ibis in the field, rev. implements of Worship within a wreath of olive, IMPER ; and others ; ex. fine valuable lot. 4 pieces

2 7 680 ANTESTIA, and unclassified (2 of the former). Good lot.
6 pieces

25 681 BAEBIA. Head of Rome, TAMPIL ; rev. Quadriga driven by Apollo, M. BAEBI. Varieties, same type with others. Unclassified, good. 6 pieces

2 0 682 CALPURINA. Head of Apollo ; rev. horseman riding at full speed, L PISO FRVGI. Varieties, with unclassified denarii ; (one very rare, cock under a bigae), all fair.
6 pieces

150 683 CAESIA. Bust of a young man launching a triple javelin, his back towards the observer ; rev. two figues seated, between them a dog, which one caresses, above the dog a head of Vulcan with pincers, L CAESI, large and extremely fine Coin. very rare ; with one of the Cassia and Cloulia families. 4 pieces

20 684 CLAUDIA ; rev. PVLCHER. Cupid, etc. Good lot. 6 ps
15 685 CORNELIA ; rev. rudder and sceptre, C. N. LEN, and others. (one plated). 6 pieces

12 686 CORDIA. Heads of the Dioscuri ; rev. Justice blindfold, with balance and hasta (misstruck), etc. ; fair. 5 pcs

22 687 CASSIA. Veiled head (Vesta) ; behind lamp : rev. Longinus standing beside an altar in the act of sacrificing ; with fine Coins of the *Astia* and *Cloulia* families. Extra fine and rare lot. 4 pieces

20 688 FABIA. Head of a female veiled ; rev. victory in a biga, in the field an Ibis, C . FABI, etc. ; very fine. 2 pieces

22 689 FANNIA ; rev. Quadriga, M . FAN - C . F ; fine and very rare.

17 690 FLAMINIA. Winged head of Pallas, behind, ROMA ; rev. victory in a biga, L FLAMIN - CILO. Extra fine with one of the *Hosidia* gems. Boar at bay ; fair.
3 pieces

15 691 FURIA. Head of Ianus. M. FOVRI - LF ; rev. Pallas crowning a trophy. One rev. - CENSOR, Silenus with skin bottle of wine ; and one of the Julia gems (broken), etc. 4 pieces

27 692 JULIA. Head of Venus ; rev. Æneas with Anchises on his shoulder, the palladium in his right hand, CAESAR. Another, rev. Quad L-JVL . BVRSI. One very fine, and both rare. 2 pieces

20 693 JUNIA. Obv. head of Pallas ; rev. SILANVS ; very fine.

694 LICINIA. Obv. same as 683; rev. Quadriga, C LICINIVS, and another. 3 pieces

695 —— Diademed and laureated head of Juno, with necklace and ear-rings, S. C.; rev. a man standing beside his horse, his armor on the ground. P. CRASSVS. M . F.; very beautiful and rare, with one of *Lucretia* gems, TRIO; with Coins of the Minucia and Marcia gens. 4 pieces

696 MARCIA. Head of Ancus Marcius in bandalet; lituus and ANCVS behind; rev. equestrian statue on a bridge, A - Q - VA - M in the arches. Another; rev. statue as before, PHILIPPVS. One with two ears of wheat, below the horses, etc.; very good and rare lot. 4 pieces

697 MINUCIA. Head of Rome; rev. the Dioscuri, R . MINV, and others pierced. 6 pieces

698 NAEVIA AND NORBANAE; fair. 4 pieces

699 PORCIA, POSTUMIA, PROCILIA, etc.; fair. 6 pieces

700 PAPIRA AND PETILLIA (the former by *Carbo*). On the latter a temple with six columns and statues; both very fine and rare. 2 pieces

701 POBLICIA and Porcia (the latter plated), with unclassified and poor. 10 pieces

702 POSTUMIA and Porcia (Coins of Albinus and Cato), the former with head of Diana and attributes; rev. three cavaliers covered with their shields, riding down an enemy; the last, with young female head, hair in net; rev. "VICTRIX," Victory seated; both extremely fine. 2 pieces

703 RENIA AND RUBRIA (rev. DOSSEN); ordinary. 4 pieces

704 SERGIA AND SCRIBONIA. Head of Pallas; rev. M - Sergia Silus, with his sword and human head in his left hand. Diademed head of Fortune; rev. an altar. PVTEAL - SCRIBON; very fine. 2 pieces

705 SERVILIA. Rev. the Dioscuri mounted, their horses starting in opposite directions, and others of the Spurillia gens. 5 pieces

706 TITURIA AND TITIA. (Rape of the Sabines, etc.) 2 pieces

707 VETURIA. Head of Rome; rev. a man on one knee holding a sow by the legs, a man standing on each side, (the "Alliance" type); and one of the VOLTEIA gens, A cock behind a helmeted female head; rev. Cybele drawn by two lions, etc. Very good and rare lot. 4 pieces

708 A fine Coin of the TULLIA family, overlooked, and others. 4 pieces

ROMAN IMPERIAL COINS.
Silver.

709 AUGUSTUS. Two reverses, his grandsons and SPQR CLV on a shield; rare, the former fine. 2 pieces

710 TIBERIUS; rev. Julia seated (tribute penny), with a duplicate of Augustus; both fine. 2 pieces

711 —— Rev. head radiated of Augustus. Another "tribute penny," and one gilt. 3 pieces

712 NERO; rev. Concordia. Extremely fine and rare, and one rev. SALVS, fair. 2 pieces

713 OTHO; rev. SECVRITAS, female standing, holding a crown and hasta; *ex. fine and rare.*

714 —— Rev. Equity standing, holding a balance and hasta, obv. fine; very rare, with a counterfeit of the type described in No. 713. 2 pieces

715 VITELLIUS; rev. dolphin on a tripod, below a raven; poor, very rare.

716 VESPASIAN; rev. "Judea," female (Judea) seated behind a trophy; plated, but antique; fine, very rare.

717 —— Two other rare types, one ex. fine. 2 pieces

718 TITUS; rev. Caducius; fair.

719 DOMITIAN. Good. 3 pieces

720 NERVA; rev. two hands clasped, CONCORDIA EXERCITVM. Ex fine, scarce.

721 —— Duplicate of last, and another. FORTVNA AVGVSTA, both fine, scarce. 2 pieces

722 TRAJAN. Interesting variety of reverses, no duplicates; fine lot. 6 pieces

723 HADRIAN. Various reverses; good lot. 5 pieces

724 —— Rev. RESTVTITORI HISPANIA, the emperor, in a toga, extending his hand to the Province, personified as a female, with a rabbit; very fine and rare.

725 SABINA (wife of Hadrian); obv. head, hair coifed in a long twist hanging down behind; rev. Venus standing; ex. fine, rare.

726 AELIUS; rev. Concord seated, R. 4; fine example.

727 ANTONINUS PIUS; rev. DIVI AVG REST COS IIII, two figures seated in an *octostyle* temple; very fine, R. 3, Well. No. 10,899.

728 —— Various reverses, fine. 4 pieces

729 MARCUS AURELIUS. Different reverses, fine. 2 pieces

730 LUCIUS VERUS; rev. Providence standing; good, scarce.

Roman Imperial Coins.

731 LUCILLA (wife of L. Verus); rev. DIANA LVCIFERA. Diana standing, holding a torch; fine, and one of Commodus. 3 pieces

732 PERTINAX; rev. female with cornucopia; only fair, rare.

733 SEPTIMUS SEVERUS; different reverses; poor. 2 pieces

734 JULIA DOMNA (wife, etc.), with *his* sons, Geta and Caracalla; all extremely fine, beautiful. 6 pieces

735 PLAUTILLA (wife of Caracalla); rev. "VENUS VICTRIX." Extremely fine, very rare.

736 ELAGABALUS; rev. PROVID . DEORVM. Ex. fine, with Julia Soaemias, his mother, and Maesa, his aunt, all as fine as when struck; very rare lot. 3 pieces

737 DIADUMENIANUS; rev. PRIN - IVVENTVTIS. The prince standing in a military habit, holding a military ensign in his right hand and hasta in his left; by his side, two other standards. Extremely fine and rare.

738 PERTINAX. Two false coins, with one of Maesa (genuine), and others doubtful. 5 pieces

739 JULIA MAMAEA, OTACILLA, and ETRUSCILLA. Superb lot. 6 pieces

740 TREBONIANUS GALLUS, Philip, Gordian III., and Trajanus Decius; very fine lot. 4 pieces

741 PHILIP II., Postumus, etc.; fine. 6 pieces

742 MISCELLANEOUS. Indifferent lot. 10 pieces

743 FLORIANUS, GRATIANUS, CLAUDIUS, etc., etc.; very fine, but base. 10 pieces

Continuation of the Series in Copper.

744 Unclassified. 20 pieces
745 Similar lot. 20 pieces
746 Similar. 20 pieces
748 Similar. 20 pieces
749 Similar. 20 pieces
750 Similar. 20 pieces
751 Selected lot, better than the average. 20 pieces
752 Similar. 20 pieces
753 THEODOSIUS, ARCADIUS, HONORIUS, AURELIAN, VALENTINIAN, etc., many very scarce. 20 pieces
754 Similar lot, equally fine. Unclassified. 20 pieces
755 Another, similar. 20 pieces
756 Another, same description. 20 pieces
757 Same. 20 pieces
758 Same. 20 pieces
759 Same. 20 pieces

Roman Imperial Coins. 39

½ { 760 THEODOSIUS, and others. Many very scarce. 20 pieces
761 Same. 20 pieces
762 Same. 20 pieces
763 Same. 20 pieces
764 Same. 20 pieces
4 ½ 765 Box of old Antique Coins of the billon size. 400 pieces

Roman Coins continued.

Imperial Brass.

7 766 As, two ounce size; Janus head; rev. prow. Poor to fair. 7 pieces
2c 767 —— Better lot. 6 pieces
12 768 AUGUSTUS, TIBERIUS, and GALBA; second size, fair lot, rare. 5 pieces
15 769 AGRIPPA, CLAUDIUS, CALIGULA and NERVA; fine lot, same size. 8 pieces
22 770 NERO, DOMITIAN, and NERVA; second size, *fine*. 5 pieces
6 771 Same. First size, poor, but rare. 3 pieces
15 772 DOMITIAN, with various reverses (second size); "Liberty," "Virtue;" The Emperor sacrificing in a hexastyle temple; "Moneta," etc. Valuable lot to a collector. 8 pieces
17 773 GERMANICUS and DRUSUS; their heads with a head of the Deified Augustus; (in good condition, and very rare); two of Antonia, and one of Germanicus. All second size, fine. 4 pieces
12 774 CLAUDIUS, with various reverses. Second size, in good order. 10 pieces
10 775 —— Similar to last, with some of Domitian; fair. 10 pieces
,, 776 HADRIAN and TRAJAN. First size, only fair. 12 pieces
17 777 Same, with rare reverses. Hadrian's voyage to Spain, Trajan's bridge over the Danube, etc.; very fair, (first size). 6 pieces
6 778 Same. Second size, rare reverses. Horse running, warrior and two trophies, Salus, etc.; fair condition. 10 pieces
5 779 Another lot, same size. 20 pieces
5 780 Same. First size, poor. 12 pieces
1,75 781 TITUS; rev. "Judea Capta;" a palm tree; to left, arms, to right, female seated; second size, fine, very rare.
20 782 VESPASIAN. First brass. "Judea Capta;" poor, rare.
6 783 VESPASIAN and TITUS. Second size, fair.
6 784 ANTONINUS PIUS. First brass, ordinary. 10 pieces
6 785 Same, with Faustina. (First and second). 10 pieces

40   *Roman Imperial Coins.*

5   786 MARCUS AURELIUS. First size.   10 pieces
5   787 Same, with Ant. Pius. and the Faustinas; poor.   20 pieces
6   788 Same. Second size.   40 pieces
15   789 CRISPINA, Lucilla, and Julia Mamaea, all first brass and fine Coins.   3 pieces
40   790 PLOTINA (wife of Trajan); DIVA PLAVTINA; rev. female standing. First brass. A piece cut off under the bust. Not much worn. R. 6.
87   791 MANLIA SCANTILLA (wife of Didius Julianus). First brass; rev. JVNO REGINA, Juno standing attended by a peacock · in fine condition, although the planchet is not quite full. Extremely rare.
7   792 LUCILLA, Crispina, Faustina, etc. First brass. Ordinary, with others, unclassified.   25 pieces
50   793 MATIDA (daughter of Marciana Trajan's sister); a rare first bronze, patinated, but not very fine.
9   794 GORDIAN III., Alexander, Philip, etc., etc., many very fine, all first brass.   60 pieces
10   795 BYZANTINE EMPERORS. Justinus and Sophia, John Zimisces, Andronicas. Good lot.   20 pieces
6²   796 MISCELLANEOUS and unclassified, all antique.   200 pieces
5   797 Same.   134 pieces
9   798 Selected and rare.   17 pieces
150   799 W. S. LINCOLN & SON's Catalogue. Half morocco.

ADDENDA TO PART I.

American Silver Dollars.

1.75	800	1795. Fillet head; ~~very fine,~~ scarce.
1.00	801	1796. Same (only type), rubbed. *Poor.*
3.25	802	1797. Seven Stars before the face of Liberty; *extremely fine, rare.*
1.25	803	1798. Large Eagle reverse; only fair. *Poor*
1.05	804	1799. Six Stars before the head, etc.; very fine.
1.15	805	1800. In ordinary condition.
3.40	806	1801. ~~Uncirculated~~, only slight hair lines produced by carelessness; *very rare.* *included all over*
1.75	807	1802. Good impression; scarce.
1.50	808	1803. In ordinary condition.
1.12	809	1840. Same description.
1.62	810	1841. Fine, scarce.
1.50	811	1842. Equally fine.
1.75	812	1843. Same.
1.75	813	1844. Same.
1.25	814	1845. ~~Same.~~
1.10	815	1846. ~~Same.~~
1.75	816	1847. ~~Extremely fine~~, scarce.
1.20	817	1848. ~~Very fine.~~
1.75	818	1849. Very fine, but little circulated.
1.10	819	1850. Poor.
2.12	820	1853. ~~Extremely~~ fine, very scarce.
1.75	821	1859. Brilliant proof.
1.50	822	1860. Same.

Half Dollars.

1.25	823	1795. ~~Extremely fine~~; rare in this condition. *fair*
2.75	824	1801. *Very* fine for date, and very scarce.
2.50	825	1802. Fine and scarce.
1.00	826	1803. ~~Almost~~ uncirculated; scarce.
.60	827	1806. ~~Very~~ fine.
.50	828	1807. ~~Same.~~
.60	829	1808. ~~Equally fine.~~

Addenda.

7s	830	1809. ~~Extremely~~ fine.	
60	831	1810. ~~Fine.~~	
55	832	1811. ~~Fine.~~	
55	833	1812. ~~Extremely~~ fine.	
6c	834	1813. Ordinary.	
137	835	1815. ~~Very fine.~~	
6c	836	1817. ~~Nearly uncirculated.~~	
"	837	1818. ~~Equally fine, brilliant.~~	
55	838	1819. ~~Fine.~~	
"	839	1820–21–22–23 and '24, all circulated.	5 pieces
65	840	1825. Two varieties, ~~extremely~~ fine.	2 pieces
55	841	1826. Ordinary.	
65	842	1827. ~~Brilliant, uncirculated~~, slight scratch.	
55	843	1829. ~~Brilliant, uncirculated.~~	
"	844	1830. Fine.	
"	845	1831. ~~Extremely~~ fine.	
"	846	1832. ~~Equally fine.~~	2 pieces
65	847	1833. Two varieties, ~~fine.~~	2 pieces
55	848	1835. ~~Extremely fine.~~	
"	849	1836. Two varieties, fair.*	2 pieces
"	850	1838. ~~Uncirculated~~, scarce.	
"	851	1839. Fine.	
"	852	1840–41–42 and '43, ~~fine.~~	4 pieces
"	853	1844 and 1849, very ~~fine.~~	2 pieces
"	854	1850–52–53–54–55–57 and '58, fair.	7 pieces
"	855	1859. Tarnished proof.	
7c	856	1860. ~~Brilliant proof.~~	
55	857	1861 and '66, fine.	2 pieces

Quarter Dollars.

32	858	1805–22–25–28; ordinary.	4 pieces
30	859	1831–32–33–34–35–36–37 and '38, mostly fine.	8 pieces
"	860	1840–45–46 and '47, fair to ~~fine.~~	4 pieces
25	861	1853–54–55–56 and '58, same.	5 pieces
35	862	1859. Brilliant proof.	
27	863	1873. Very fine.	

Dimes.

175	864	1796. ~~Fine~~, rare.	
40	865	1809. ~~Fine~~, scarce.	
3c	866	1821. Nearly uncirculated, very rare in this condition.	
2c	867	1834. ~~Equally fine~~, scarce.	
1c	868	1820–25–27–28–29–30–31–33–35–38–39–41–46, etc.; ordinary.	16 pieces

Half Dimes and Three Cents.

80	869	1797. Fine for date, scarce.	
100	870	1800. ~~Very fine.~~	

Addenda. 43

5	871	1829 and 1830, fine; 1831 and '32, very fine; 1833 and '34, fair; 1835 and '6, very good, and 1839, poor. 9 pcs
10	872	1840. *Uncirculated*, rare.
2	873	1842-43-44 and '47, ordinary. 4 pieces
5	874	1845 ~~Uncommonly fine~~, rare.
5	875	Various dates in the fifties and sixties, generally fine, with nickel, 1868 and '69. 11 pieces
5	876	1859. Fine proof, scarce.
6	877	Three Cents of various early dates, with proofs of 1859 and '60.

Cents and Half Cents.

3s	878	1794 and '96 (fillet head), the former plugged. 2 pieces
8c	879	1800, 1806 and 1807, the "6" a pretty good Cent. 3 pcs
5 oc	880	1801. ~~Extremely fine~~, rare.
5 cc	881	1804. Broken die, ~~hardly circulated~~, but dark; ~~fine sharp impression~~ and desirable.
30	882	1808-11 and '13, fair cents. 3 pieces
100	883	1809. ~~Very fine~~ for date, dark, rare.
3 o	884	1810. ~~Equally fine~~, dark, scarce.
25	885	1821-22-23-24, all scarce and ~~fine~~. 4 pieces
6 c	886	1835 and Massachusetts Cent of 1787, both fine. 2 pieces
2	887	Cents of various dates; ordinary. 53 pieces
20	888	Half Cent, 1806; brilliant.
3	889	—— 1809-28-35-50-53-56 and '57, all extremely fine, and one of 1804, poor. 8 pieces
70	890	—— 1833. Brilliant; uncirculated.
100	891	—— 1834. Brilliant; proof, rare.

105	892	Gold California Dollar, 1860.

7s	893	Tunis Dollars. Slightly debased silver. 2 pieces
8	894	Russian, French, and English Silver Coins, etc. (Intrinsic value, 75 cts.) 7 pieces
8 o	895	Tempo (Japan), Spanish *weights* and modern Shekel (tin); very fine lot. 4 pieces
4c	896	Ancient large bronze Coins of Egypt. 3 pieces
13	897	Greek of Agathocles, very *fine*; and several other fine, and as many poor antiques. Unclassified. 16 pieces
2	898	String of Chinese Cash and modern copper Coins. 54 pieces
1	899	Base, and uncirculated copper Coins. 12 pieces

End of Part I.

PART II.

[Another Property.]

Silver Medals.

8,5c   900 RELIGIOUS MEDAL by C. D. The three kings, Balthasar, Caspar, and Melchior, doing homage and presenting gifts to the infant Christ; stable with accessories; rev. child nimbused surrounded by clouds within two circles of ins. and border; edge lettered and date 1793; beautiful.   Size 36

25c   901 BAPTISMAL. John Baptizing Christ; Scripture-texts in Dutch; extremely fine.   Size 34

150   902 The same, different design, old medal; worn and pierced.   Size 32

125   903 RELIGIOUS; scene in a temple; rev. large nude figure to the middle, body covered with sores, Dutch ins. on both sides; gilt medal, with loop.   Size 30

76   904 —— Bust of Christ; quotation from John XIV., ins. in Dutch.   Size 25

175   905 REFORMATION Jubilee Medal; busts of Luther and Melancthon; rev. church at Augsburg, ins. 1530–1830; very fine and rare.   Size 22

62   906 —— To commemorate the festival in Bern, 1828; open Bible surrounded by rays and ins.   Size 16

35   906* PIUS VII.; rev. Crucifixion, companion; oval medalets. Size 16.   2 pieces

45   907 LARGE oval medallions, with loops; weight one ounce.   2 pieces

55c   908 VENETIÆ; view of the city, "VRBVM REGINA"; rev. the city sitting as a queen, attendants displaying a map of the "MOREA"; edge lettered; extremely fine.   Size 32

9.c o   909 GUSTAVUS ADOLPHUS, bust; rev. PEPIGIT NOBIS HAEC FOEDERA VICTOR; two female figures, one with a cross; beautiful proof medal, rare.   Size 28

5 c   910 CHARLES XIII., coronation medal, 1809.   Size 20

6 c   911 CHARLES XIV. (Sweden), bust; rev. ploughman turning furrows.   Size 20

Bronze Medals.

7 5   912 CHARLES XV., bust; rev. within wreath LAND SKAL MED LOV BYGGES; proof.   Size 20

7 5   913 OSCAR I. (Sweden), bust; rev. an edifice, "UPPLATET D, 8 Aug. 1859"; fine proof.   Size 20

1 10   914 MARRIAGE Medal by *Pingrel*, bride and groom at a Christian altar; rev. beautiful wreath of roses surrounding a plain field.   Size 26

3 0   915 WATERLOO Medalet of George, Prince Regent, bust; rev. "Wellington, Waterloo," Victory seated; fine and rare.   Size 14

4 0 c   916 NAPOLEON III., Mexican war medal, with loop, by *Barre*.   Size 20

8 5   917 PRIZE and commemorative medals of uniform size and merit, all extremely fine, RENNT BRVDER EURE MACHT SIE LIEGT, etc.—HENRICVS WREDE CENTVRIO, etc.; and two others. Size 21.   4 pieces

25   918 Similar in character, smaller size.   4 pieces

22   919 CALLAO Medalet, 28 July, 1862, EL PERU LIBRE; inauguration of a R R in Arequipa (S. A.), 1871; American Congress in Lima, 1864, and coronation medal, Fred. Christ., 1747; beautiful lot. Size 16.   4 pieces

45   920 PROMULGADA en Lima, 1860, of the Constitution, similar of Ferd. VII. in 1808, by ORRUTIA, MANUD PARDO, Pres., etc., 1872, and an old medal of Melgaredo and Munoz; all South American and uncommon; half-dollar size.   4 pieces

3 50   921 UNITED STATES Agricultural Society prize medal, by *Mitchell*, "Awarded to Chapman & May," Chicago, 1859; superb proof.   Size 48

15   922 ENGRAVED lozenge-shaped medal, religious.

Bronze Medals.

1 00   923 ANTONIUS OTTHO BON. CAP. GEN. S. R. E.; bust in wig; rev. a car in the air drawn by a winged lion (Itmares) and bitch wolf (Rome), destruction and death in the clouds, and on the sea below, CIVITATES IMPIORVM DESTRVET DNS ET LATOS FACIET, etc., by GIOS ORTOI, of admirable work, cast in high relief, carefully finished and plated.   Size 48

25   924 MEDAL of the same size, cast in iron, head, side only; one smaller of Louis XIV., and one of Louis Philippi; all iron.   3 pieces

46   *Bronze Medals.*

- *1 2*   925 CHARLES XI., Sweden; cast oval Dutch medal of 1695, and ditto Swedish of Ulric Eleonore, etc.; uncommon old bronzes, poor.   4 pieces
- *115*   926 CAROLO JOHANNI D. G. REGI NORV. SVEC. GOTH, etc., laureated bust; rev. PRISCVM NIDAROSIAE DECVS, etc.; the king on his throne, etc., etc.; splendid proof.   Size 40
- *175*   927 —— Duplicate, equally fine.
- *"*   927* NAPOLEON BONAPARTE, laureated bust; rev. TVTELA PRAESENS, the emperor seated, Genius standing; splendid proof.   Size 44
- *3 5*   928 LOUIS XV., bust; rev. SPES ALTERA REGNI; rev. Hope holding two wreaths, nuptials of Charles Ferd. and Caroline; very fine.   Size 32
- *13 c*   929 LOUIS XVIII.; rev. GALLIA ET AMERICA FOEDERATA; the two nations personified, etc., 1822; fine proof, and rare.   Size 32
- *115*   930 WM. CAMDEN, Queen Caroline (Eng.), prize medal by *Looz*, Charles and Louisa of Sweden by same, and King George "Preserved from Assassination," May 15, 1800; extremely fine medals. Size 28.   5 pieces
- *80*   931 NAPOLEON III. and Eugenie; rev. the birth of the Prince; fine proof, by *Montagny*.   Size 34
- *60*   932 VICTOR EMANUEL, by *Hart;* rev. arms; fine proof.   Size 38
- *3 c*   933 PAPAL; Paul V., Urban VIII., and Sixtus IV.; fine; and one of St. Charles Bar.   4 pieces
- *15*   934 MICHAD, SKJELDERUP Dr., etc., by *Looz*, and other fine medals, same character, *e. g.* Henry IV. and Louis XVIII., Charles X., etc., etc. Size 22.   6 pieces
- *5*   935 —— Another lot, not as fine, but uncommon, as one to commemorate the Reformation Jubilee, Geneve, 1834; same size as last.   6 pieces
- *20*   936 CHARLES GUSTAVUS (Sweden), 1660; beautiful medal in Berlin iron, and another in same metal.   2 pieces
- *7²*   937 NAPOLEON III. (on his election and as Emperor), a medal struck in Lima, French (Monneron's tokens), etc.; about size 20.   8 pieces
- *4*   938 ENGLISH; Henry IV., Ed. VI., and others of Frederic the Great; poor lot.   8 pieces
- *1 c*   939 LOUIS XVIII., Souvenir de L'Exposition Universelle Calendar, 1805; medal of Charles XII., Sweden, etc.; av. size 32; good lot.   6 pieces
- *4*   940 NEW YORK Crystal Palace medal, poor; one of the French Exposition ditto, and one of same in lead, fine. 3 pieces

Medalets, Meraux, and Jetons.

941 MEDALETS in fine brass, mostly French and with loops, no duplicates; extremely fine lot; many souvenirs of the Exposition. 10 pieces

942 ——— Similar lot, with others of a religious character. 10 pieces

943 ——— Old religious and jetons, poor. 10 pieces

944 ——— Extremely small fine medalets, with loops; rare lot. 17 pieces

945 A similar lot, without loops, not as fine, with jetons of a miscellaneous character, but generally with heads; ordinary. 20 pieces

945* Another lot, selected and fine. 10 pieces

946 OLD money weights, etc. 10 pieces

947 MERAUX of the XVIIIth Century, interesting; generally size 18. 10 pieces

948 NUREMBERG jetons, thin brass. 15 pieces

949 FRENCH jetons and medalets in copper, with fine designs and in good preservation; average size 18; valuable lot. 10 pieces

950 BRASS medalets, with heads of royal and distinguished persons, as George III. and Charlotte, Field Marshal Blucher, etc., etc. Size 16. 10 pieces

951 Similar with others, without heads, copper and brass; good lot. 10 pieces

952 JETONS, miscellaneous. 20 pieces

952* Similar lot. 30 pieces

953 SMALL and well-executed copper medals, LOUIS PHILIPPI, TROLLE, King LEOPOLD of Belgium, CHARLES XIV. of Sweden, Count WITTEMBERG, JOHN RUDBECKIUS, and NIC. ROSEN; about size 20; very fine. 7 pieces

954 Others, with and without heads; same size. 10 pieces

955 MEDALET calendar, brass; fine. 2 pieces

956 IMPRESSIONS of gems and seals from the antique in iron, various sizes; fine. 10 pieces

957 Another lot, similar; some of these have been mounted and worn as ornaments or used as seals; very fine. 10 pieces

958 MASONIC seal, extremely fine, with others similar to those described. 6 pieces

959 MISCELLANEOUS jetons and tokens in lead and brass, some found in the Rhine. 20 pieces

960 ——— Others, mostly brass. 25 pieces

48   *Store Cards, Etc.*

Tin Medals.

961 PRUSSIAN (Fred. Mag.), Saxon, old Venetian, Henry IV. (one side only), GRETRY, and old English fire-engine medal; all very old and curious; about size 24.   6 pieces

962 JOAN OF ARC, to commemorate the inauguration of a statue to her honor, 1855; fine medal.   Size 40

963 GOTTER MENKEN, Dutch religious medal, etc. Size 30.   3 pieces

964 LORD NELSON, Trafalgar; fine proof.   Size 32

965 ARTHUR, Duke of Wellington, "Died," etc., Marc Brunel; Pr. Albert, H. R. H. Prince of Wales, his visit to Canada; same, the Victoria Bridge opened, etc. Size 28.   5 pieces

966 CRYSTAL PALACE, Sydenham; opening a R. R. in S. A., 1871, FERRO CARRIL DE IQUIQUE A LA NORIA; the Great Britain, and others smaller; two largest, size 34.   7 pieces

Store Cards, Political Tokens, Public and Private Issues of Currency, etc., etc., in the United States and Colonies.

967 A COLLECTION of store cards, in which the rare Vermont token of "GUSTIN & BLAKE, tin, copper, and sheet-iron workers, Chelsea," etc., with a picture of a copper pot, will be found; without duplicates and in good condition.   30 pieces

968 SHIN-PLASTERS and store cards, unclassified, copper and brass; old U. S. cent size; no poor pieces. 100 pieces

969 Another lot, similar.   150 pieces

970 Similar, containing also a few of the half-cent size, with Dr. Feuchtwanger's cents of 1837.   125 pieces

971 ADVERTISING Cards, containing United States postage-stamps of the denomination of 10, 5, 3, and 1 cents, the first two being Gage, Brother & Drake's, Chicago, the others Dr. Ayers', on which we are strongly recommended to try his pills; now rare (the cards).   15 pieces

972 COLLECTION of copperheads, generally bright. 700 pieces

973 WOOD'S tokens, 1723; North American do., 1781; Talbot, Allum & Lee, 1794, and Virginia cents; very good lot.   8 pieces

974 —— Repetition of last, fair to poor.   8 pieces

975 LOUISIANA, Vermont, New Jersey, Franklin, with a repetition of 974; from fair to poor.   25 pieces

United States Silver Coins.

¼   976 Another lot of about the same description and quality.
                                                                                                                                 40 pieces

14   977 NOVA-CONSTELLATIO, Nova-Eborac (two varieties), Fugio's, New Jersey, and Vermon-Auctori's ; generally fine.
                                                                                                                          12 pieces

2h   978 VERMONTENSIUM, Vermon-Auctori, and Rosa-Americana half-penny ; fair condition and scarce.   3 pieces

3s   979 MASSACHUSETTS cents, 1787 and 1788 ; very good.   2 pieces

4s   980 Same, with half-cents, 1788 ; good.   4 pieces

10   981 MASSACHUSETTS button, cents, Rosa-Americana, and Nova-Constellatio ; from good to poor.   12 pieces

5   982 MASSACHUSETTS and Nova-Constellatio, poor.   22 pieces

6   983 CONNECTICUT, Massachusetts, and Nova-Constellatio, many varieties of the first ; ordinary.   20 pieces

3½   984 CONNECTICUTS, poor to fair.   63 pieces

12   985 Same (selected), 1785, 1786, 1787, with the varieties ET LIB INDE, and one with horn on armor ; good lot.
                                                                                                                           6 pieces

1   986 POLITICAL and temperance medalets and tokens of Van Buren, Harrison, Lincoln, Jackson, Clay, Fremont' Douglass, McClellan, etc. ; ordinary lot.   61 pieces

13   987 WASHINGTON cents of 1783, with and without date, double-head, *Unity* States, etc.; poor.   8 pieces

11   988 Same, fine, with Idler's copy of the half-dollar in tin.
                                                                                                                            4 pieces

1/4c   989 —— Cent of 1791, only fair ; scarce.

7s   990 —— Mint medal, " Time increases his Fame"; fine, copper.
                                                                                                                             Size 18

8   991 RELIC of the great Portland Fire, copper cents melted and cemented by silver.

UNITED STATES SILVER COINS.

Dollars.

11c   992 1795, fillet head, fair, slightly scratched.
16 2   993 1796, fine for this date.
17s   994 1797, six stars to r. of head, fair.   2 pieces
13c   995 1798, large eagle reverse, fine.
1.2c   996 1799, very fine.
1.1c   997 Same, with one of 1800, good.   2 pieces
1 2c   998 1800, fine.
1.5c   999 1802, very good.

4

1.30	1000	1840, fine.	2 pieces
1.10	1001	1841, fine.	
1.05	1002	1842, ~~very fine~~.	
,,	1003	Same, both fine.	2 pieces
1.10	1004	1843, good impression.	
1.00	1005	Same, good.	2 pieces
1.05	1006	1844, pierced.	
,,	1007	1846, ~~fine~~.	
1.00	1008	1846, both ~~fine~~.	2 pieces
,,	1009	1847, ~~fine~~.	
,,	1010	Same, ordinary.	2 pieces
1.30	1011	1860, very fine.	
1.05	1012	Same, both fine.	2 pieces
1.15	1013	1861, very fine.	
1.05	1014	Same, both fine.	2 pieces
1.25	1015	1862, extremely fine.	
1.05	1016	Same, equally fine.	2 pieces
1.40	1017	1863, very fine.	
1.05	1018	Same, equally fine.	2 pieces
1.05	1019	1868, fine.	
1.10	1020	1869, very fine.	
1.05	1021	1871, fine.	2 pieces
1.25	1022	1873, ~~fine~~.	2 pieces

Half-Dollars.

1.30	1022*	1794, ~~fair impression~~ and scarce. 1.5	
1.00	1023	1795, very good impression, fine for date.	
.55	1024	Same, very ~~fair~~.	2 pieces
.60	1025	1803, very good, of 1795.	2 pieces
	1026	Same, both 1803 and 1795; very fair.	2 pieces
	1027	1805 and 1806, good examples.	2 pieces
.55	1028	1806, two varieties, fine.	2 pieces
	1029	Same, two varieties, the pointed and knotted 6; fair.	2 pieces
	1030	Same, pointed date, good.	2 pieces
.70	1031	1807, varieties, head right and same left; fine, scarce.	2 pieces
.55	1032	Same, the two varieties repeated, fair.	2 pieces
.55	1033	1808, fine, with one of 1807; fair.	2 pieces
.80	1034	1809, *extremely* fine, scarce.	
.55	1035	Same, with one of 1808, fair.	2 pieces

United States Silver Coins. 51

55	⎧ 1036	1809, both of this date, very fine.	2 pieces
	⎪ 1037	1810, fine, with one of 1809, fine.	2 pieces
	⎨ 1038	Same, with one of 1811, fine.	2 pieces
	⎪ 1039	Repetition of last (1810 and 1811).	2 pieces
	⎩ 1040	1811, very good, with one of 1812, good.	2 pieces
85	1041	1812, *very fine*, scarce.	
55	⎧ 1042	Same, fine.	2 pieces
	⎪ 1043	1813 and 1814, very good impressions.	2 pieces
	⎨ 1044	1817, die altered from 1815; fine and scarce.	
	⎪ 1045	Same, two varieties, very fine.	2 pieces
	⎪ 1046	1818, with one of 1817, extremely fine.	2 pieces
	⎩ 1047	Same, both of this date, very fine.	2 pieces
6c	1048	1819, with one of 1818, very fine.	2 pieces
55	1049	Same, both dates repeated, fine.	2 pieces
80	1050	1820, very fine (die of 1819), scarce.	
65	1051	Same, two varieties, fine.	2 pieces
,,	1052	1821, uncirculated, rare.	
55	1053	Same, with one of 1819; both fine.	2 pieces
60	1054	1822, extremely fine, scarce.	
,,	1055	Same, with one of 1821; very fine.	2 pieces
55	1056	1823, with one of 1822; very good.	2 pieces
6c	1057	Same, fine.	2 pieces
7c	1058	1824, uncirculated, brilliant, scarce.	
55	1059	Same, with 1823; very fine.	2 pieces
60	1060	1825, nearly uncirculated, ex. fine.	
55	⎧ 1061	Same, very fine.	2 pieces
	⎨ 1062	Same, with 1824; fine.	2 pieces
	1063	1826, uncirculated, scarce.	
	⎪ 1064	Same, nearly uncirculated.	2 pieces
	⎩ 1065	Same, with one of 1825; all fine.	3 pieces
7c	1066	1827, uncirculated, brilliant, stars pointed; scarce.	
60	1067	Same, uncirculated, different die.	
55	1068	Same, brilliant.	2 pieces
,,	1069	Same, with one of 1826; very fine.	2 pieces
6c	1070	Same, with one of 1828; both brilliant.	2 pieces
60	1071	1828, uncirculated.	
55	1072	Same, with one of 1829; very fine.	2 pieces
6c	1073	Repetition of last.	2 pieces
55	1074	1829, with one of 1830; very fine.	2 pieces
,,	1075	Repetition of last.	2 pieces
65	1076	1830, brilliant, uncirculated.	

United States Silver Coins.

1077	1830, brilliant, uncirculated, with one of 1831; equally fine.	2 pieces
1078	1831, extremely fine.	2 pieces
1079	Same, with one of 1832; very fine.	2 pieces
1080	Repetition of last.	2 pieces
1081	1832, very fine, with one of 1833.	2 pieces
1082	Same repeated.	2 pieces
1083	1833, extremely fine.	2 pieces
1084	1834, large and small date, ex. fine.	2 pieces
1085	Same repeated, equally fine.	2 pieces
1086	1835, with one of 1834, small date; very fine.	2 pieces
1087	Same, extremely fine.	2 pieces
1088	1836, with one of 1835; very fine.	2 pieces
1089	Same, all fine, and '36.	3 pieces
1090	1837, uncirculated.	
1091	Same, fine.	2 pieces
1092	1838, very fine and fine.	3 pieces
1093	1839, fine.	2 pieces
1094	1840, very fine.	2 pieces
1095	1841 and 1842, very fine.	2 pieces
1096	1843, very fine.	2 pieces
1096*	1844, very fine, with one of '43.	2 pieces
1097	Repetition of last, equally fine.	2 pieces
1098	1845, fine, with one of 1844.	2 pieces
1099	1846 and 1847, fine.	2 pieces
1100	1859, with one of 1863; very fine.	2 pieces
1101	1863, uncirculated, brilliant.	2 pieces
1102	Same, equally fine.	2 pieces
1103	1865, very fine, with one of 1863.	2 pieces
1104	1866, uncirculated, with one of 1863.	2 pieces
1105	Same, uncirculated (both '66).	2 pieces
1106	1867, brilliant proof, rare.	
1107	Same, uncirculated, with one of '66.	2 pieces
1108	1868, uncirculated.	2 pieces
1109	1873, one uncirculated.	2 pieces

Proof Sets.

1110	1860, brilliant. (7 pieces)	
1111	1863, same.	
1112	1864, same. (9 pieces)	
1113	1865, same. (8 pieces)	

United States Silver Coins.

3 25	1114	1866, brilliant. (9 pieces)	
3 25	1115	Same repeated.	
10	1116	Same, proof pattern 5 cents nickel, shield, "In God we Trust"; rev. "5" in rays and stars, brilliant. 2 pieces	
3 0	1117	Repetition of last.	4 pieces
3 25	1118	1867, brilliant proof set. (10 pieces)	
3s c	1119	Same, duplicate set.	
5 0	1120	Same, small set proofs. (4 pieces)	
4 c	1121	Duplicate, small set.	
3s 0	1122	1868, brilliant proof set. (10 pieces)	
2 50	1123	Same, duplicate.	
2 7s	1124	1869, brilliant proof set. (10 pieces)	
2s 0	1125	Same, duplicate set.	

Quarter-Dollars.

6 0	1126	1796, considerably rubbed and partly pierced; rare.	
5 J	1127	——— same condition, pierced.	
3 s	1128	1804, poor, pierced; rare. 9¢	
//	1129	1805, fair, scarce. 5 c	
//	1130	——— another, rather poor.	
25	1131	1806, considerably rubbed.	
50	1132	1807, very good, scarce.	
3 s	1133	1815, much rubbed, scarce.	
5 J	1134	1818, fine.	
3 s	1135	1820, fair.	
4 c	1136	1821, fine.	
4 c	1137	1822, poor, scarce.	
2	1138	1831, fine.	
25	1139	1834, fine.	
//	1140	1835, very fine.	
6 c	1141	1836, fine.	
25	1142	1837, fair.	
3 s	1143	1851, '52, '53, and '58, fine.	4 pieces
2/	1144	1861 and '62, very fine.	2 pieces
4 c	1145	1862, uncirculated.	4 pieces
3 s	1146	1863, uncirculated, beautiful.	2 pieces
3 c	1147	——— repetition, beautiful.	2 pieces
4 c	1148	1864, '65, '66, and '69, uncirculated.	4 pieces
//	1149	1868, uncirculated.	
//	1150	1873, without arrow-heads, with date, uncirculated; rare.	
3 0	1151	——— with arrows, uncirculated.	3 pieces

Dimes.

11	1152	1800, '01, and '05, very poor.	10 pieces
15	1153	1805, good impression for date, scarce.	
11	1154	—— from poor to good.	3 pieces
10	1155	1807, all poor.	4 pieces
10	1156	1811 and '14, poor.	5 pieces
15	1157	1814, good and fair.	3 pieces
12	1158	1820 and '21, very good.	2 pieces
10	1159	Same (1820 and '21), poor.	3 pieces
15	1160	1823, very good for date.	
12	1161	1823, '24, and '25, ordinary.	3 pieces
	1162	1825, very good impression, with one of 1827 and '28; good lot.	4 pieces
	1163	1829, fine, and 1831 and '34 equally so.	3 pieces
	1164	1835, '37, '38, '39, '41, and '42; good lot.	6 pieces
	1165	1843, '45, '46, '48, and '49; very fair.	5 pieces
20	1166	1846, very good for date, scarce.	
10	1167	1853, with and without arrows, fine.	4 pieces
	1168	—— same, without arrows, fair.	5 pieces
	1169	—— with 1855 and '56, very fine.	3 pieces
	1170	1856 and '59, good to fair.	4 pieces
15 20	1171	1860, uncirculated, brilliant.	5 pieces
20	1172	1863, brilliant proofs, scarce.	4 pieces
20	1173	Same, with 1864, '65, and '66; all brilliant proofs.	4 pieces
15	1174	Repetition of last, equally fine.	4 pieces
1/2	1175	Another lot of these fine proofs, same dates.	7 pieces
	1176	1867, '68, and '69, brilliant proofs.	10 pieces
	1177	—— same dates, equally fine.	10 pieces
	1178	1873, without arrow-heads, uncirculated.	2 pieces
	1179	Same, with arrows, uncirculated.	2 pieces

Half-Dimes.

10	1180	1795 and 1800, pierced and poor.	6 pieces
12	1181	1800, very fair impression, scarce.	
10	1182	1829, '31, '32, '35, '37 (two varieties), fine.	6 pieces
7 1/2	1183	1829, '32, '35, '36; all fine.	6 pieces
"	1184	1840, '42, '43, '44, 47, and '49; very good lot.	6 pieces
55	1185	1846, good for date, rare.	
10	1186	1844, '50, and '53; indifferent lot.	10 pieces

United States Silver Coins. 55

	1187	1853 (two varieties), '54, '57, '58, and '59; all very fine. 10 pieces
10	1188	1853 and '54, from fair to fine. 6 pieces
	1189	1859, N. O. Mint, very good, and 1860, '63, '64, '65, '66, '67, '68, and '69, brilliant and uncirculated. 10 pieces
7½	1190	Same, except 1859; all brilliant. 10 pieces
	1191	Same repeated. 10 pieces
12	1192	1860, '65, '66, '67, '68, and '69; all brilliant. 12 pieces
10	1193	1866, '67, '68, '69, '70, '71, '72, and '73; uncirculated nickels (5 cts.) 8 pieces

Three-Cents.

17	1194	1851, '52, '53, '55, and '56; all fine. 10 pieces
16	1195	Same dates repeated, equally fine. 4 pieces
27	1196	1860, '62, '63, '66, and '70; uncirculated and brilliant. 15 pieces

Cents.

125	1197	1793, wreath, rubbed and dark, but *fair*; rare.
100	1198	—— variety of the same, rather poor.
3 c	1199	1794, two varieties, in ordinary condition. 2 pieces
90	1200	1795, plain edge, very good; fine for date.
11	1201	—— lettered and plain edges, poor. 3 pieces
17	1202	1796, Liberty cap and wreath, rather poor. 3 pieces
50	1203	1797 and 1798, very good impressions. 2 pieces
1 c	1204	—— same, poor. 2 pieces
3,75	1205	1799, rather poor, but undoubtedly genuine; rare.
12	1206	1800, over the '99, fair, with others, poor. 4 pieces
20	1207	1801, from fair to poor. 4 pieces
25	1208	1802, same, with one of 1803. 4 pieces
200	1209	1804, poor, scarce.
12	1210	1805, from fair to very good. 5 pieces
27	1211	1806 and 1807, with varieties same description. 7 pieces
15	1212	1808, fair for date, and poor. 2 pieces
4c	1213	1809, very poor, scarce; and 1810, good. 2 pieces
45	1214	1811, varieties, poor. 3 pieces
15	1215	1812, fair, with 1813, poor. 4 pieces
5	1216	1814, varieties, rather poor. 2 pieces
10	1217	1816, perfect and broken, dies very good. 2 pieces
"	1218	1817, 13 and 15 stars, and other varieties; fair lot. 8 pieces
12	1219	1818 and 1819, fine, varieties. 4 pieces
"	1220	1820, very fair. 2 pieces

United States Silver Coins.

5	1221	1821 and 1822, fine, but dark.	2 pieces
5	1222	—— same, poor.	2 pieces
12	1223	1823, two varieties, broken and perfect dies; poor, scarce.	
3 c	1224	1824, very fine impression, dark; scarce.	
7½	1225	1824 and '25, ordinary.	3 pieces
12	1226	1826, two varieties, fine.	2 pieces
12	1227	1827, two varieties, fine; one *very* fine.	2 pieces
5	1228	1826 and '27, fair to good.	3 pieces
2	1229	1828 and '29, ordinary.	4 pieces
10	1230	1830, very fine, dark.	
3	1231	1831 and '30, ordinary.	3 pieces
3	1232	1832 and '33, fine to fair.	4 pieces
12	1233	1834, two varieties; both fine.	2 pieces
1	1234	1835 and '36, ordinary.	3 pieces
5	1235	1836, dies broken in different places, very fine.	2 pieces
5	1236	1837, all fine, and 1838, equally fine.	7 pieces
11	1237	1839, three varieties; good lot.	5 pieces
10	1238	1840, very fine, nearly uncirculated.	
1	1239	1841 and '42, poor.	3 pieces
5	1240	1842, large and small date, fine.	2 pieces
2	1241	1843 and '44, good.	2 pieces
2	1242	1844 and '45, very fine, scarce.	2 pieces
1	1243	1845 and '46, ordinary.	4 pieces
2	1244	1847, '48, '49, all very good.	4 pieces
9	1245	1850 to 1857 inclusive, nearly all bright.	18 pieces
3	1246	Misstruck cents, planchets, brass cent of 1848, cents incused, etc.	18 pieces
4.cc	1247	1856, nickel cent, very fine, rare.	
6	1248	Uncirculated bright two cents, 1864, '65, '67, '70, '71, and '72.	11 pieces
1/	1249	Nickel and copper (same size), bright and uncirculated, from 5, to 73.	28 pieces
1/	1250	Same, brilliant proofs, 62, 63, 64, 66, and 67.	6 pieces
3	1251	Three cents, nickel, fine proofs, 1865.	4 pieces
6	1252	Others, uncirculated.	6 pieces
8	1253	Set of cents from 1793 to 1857, with all the dates except 1799 and 1804.	63 pieces
3	1254	Old cents from 1797 to 1823.	200 pieces

Half-Cents.

5	1255	1794, '97, 1800, '03, '04, '05, '06, '07, '08, '09, '10, '25, '26, '28, '29, '32, '33, '34, '35, '49, '51, '53, '55, '56, and '57; from fine to poor.	52 pieces

1256 Same, various dates, among them many in very good condition. 260 pieces

Electrotypes.

1257 TRIAL PIECE, etc., 1792; Washington cent, with the same reverse as last (a mule); Granby, Confederatio, Immunis Columbia, Sommer Islands; Pitt token, Washington half-dollar, etc., etc., etc. 18 pieces

FOREIGN SILVER COINS.
France.

1258 HENRY II. II., with crown and liles; rev. cross, Fleurie, testoon; rare.

1259 LOUIS XIIII. 1-16 crown, ex. fine, with 1-4 ditto and half do. (13-16); the lot.

1260 LOUIS XV. Quarter-crown or 20 sous, 1791; beautiful and very rare.

1261 —— Small coins of Louis XIV. and XV., some for the Provinces; rare. 9 pieces

1262 LOUIS XVI. Crown of 1786, fine; scarce.

1263 —— XXX and XX sols and 1-8 crown. 3 pieces

1264 NAPOLEON I. 5 francs, 1810 (*Tiolier*); good.

1265 LOUIS XVIII. Same, 1815; good.

1266 CHARLES X. and LOUIS XVIII. 2 and 1 francs, fine. 2 pieces

1267 REPUBLIC, 1849. Five francs, LIBERTY, EGALITE, FRATERNITE; very fine, scarce.

1268 —— One franc, uncirculated. 2 pieces

1269 NAPOLEON III. Five francs, two do. and one do., 50 centimes and 20 ditto; uncirculated and brilliant, rare. 5 pieces

1270 REPUBLIC. Five francs of 1873, same as 1267; brilliant.

Italy.

1271 VENICE. Peter Mocenigo Doge, 1474–1476, half-ducat, Duke kneeling before St. Mark, PE. MOCENIGO S. MARCVS V.; rev. Christ standing; in fine preservation and rare. Size 20

1272 LOMBARDO-VENETIO. GALEAZZO MARIA SFORZA, 1466, bust in a kind of hood; rev. winged dragon, etc.; a very fine thick coin, rare. Size 20

1273 SARDINIA. Charles Emanuel, Charles Felix, 1771 and 1825; av. third-dollar size. 3 pieces

58   *Foreign Silver Coins.*

75   1274 TUSCANY.   Leopold II. ; rev. lily ; varieties ; average quarter size ; very fine.   4 pieces
200 1275 ROME. Pius VII., scudo, uncirculated, of 1802 ; scarce.
150 1276 —— Same, of 1815 ; brilliant and beautiful.
150 1277 —— Gregory XVI., scudo of 1845 ; ex. fine.
10   1278 —— Pius X., fine uncirculated coins of 20 baiocchi, 10 do., and 10 and 5 soldi size (aggregate value, 1 dollar).   9 pieces
15   1279 Other Papal coins, unclassified, av. value 15 cents ; fair.   8 pieces
100 1280 SICILY. Ferdinand, scudo of 1796, fine and scarce.
150 1281 —— Same, with Caroline, two heads, 1791 ; fine and scarce.
11   1282 —— Ferdinand I., Infanta, bust crowned, fine scudo of 1818.
100 1283 —— Francis I., 1825, very fine scudo.
50   1284 —— Half-scudo of same, with others of Ferd. IV. ; same size.   3 pieces
11   1285 —— Unclassified, av. value about 12 cents.   14 pieces
34   1286 KINGDOM OF ITALY. Victor Emanuel, uncirculated and brilliant set of 5 lire, 2 do., 1 do., 50 centimes, and 20 do.   5 pieces
12   1287 —— Others of Victor Emanuel, 2, 1, and ½ lire.   3 pieces
110 1288 REPUBLIC OF ITALY. 5 lire of 1848, one fine.   2 pieces

Germany.

40   1289 HOLLAND. Ducatoon of Campen, 1692, with two other coins ; one a piece of 1 gulden.   3 pieces
95   1290 BRANDENBURG. Dollar of Frederick III., 1693, and a medal dollar of Alexander, 1767, with a view of the porcelain factory of Bruckberg ; very rare and very fine ; both thaler size.
35   1291 PRUSSIA. Frederick III. (the Great), thalers of 1750–1783 and third-thaler of 1771.   3 pieces
67   1292 —— Fred. William III., thaler of 1818, with one of Fred. Will. IV., 1845, very fine.   2 pieces
100 1293 —— William and William and Augusta, fine thalers, with one and two heads.   4 pieces
125 1294 AUSTRIA. Joseph II., 1788, fine crown.
60   1295 —— Francis I. and II., thalers.   2 pieces
65   1296 —— Frederick II. and Jos. II., thalers.   2 pieces
30   1297 —— Francis Jos. I., gulden and half do., fine.   2 pieces

Foreign Silver Coins. 59

- 1298 AUSTRIA. Frances I. (20 krs.), very fine. 5 pieces
- 1299 HUNGARY. Convention crown of Maria Theresa, 1766; ex. fine, rare.
- 1300 —— Crown of 1780; rev. Madonna and Jesus; very fine.
- 1301 —— ⅔ and ½ crown, and 20 and 10 krs.; fine. 5 pieces
- 1302 SAXONY. Thaler (⅔ crown) of 1590, busts of Fred. William and Johannes, brothers and dukes; rare and well preserved.
- 1303 —— John George, 1692, half-crown, fair.
- 1304 —— John V., double thaler of 1861, very fine.
- 1305 —— Half-crowns and medalet, fair. 3 pieces
- 1306 WURTEMBERG and HAMBURG. Thaler, gulden, and quarter-dollar; fair. 3 pieces
- 1307 BRUNSWICK and LUNENBURG. 24 Marien groschen or half crown of 1705, wild man of the Hartz; very fine.
- 1308 —— Convention piece (⅔ crown) of Duke Charles, 1764, with fine ⅔ crown of Geo. III. (England). 2 pieces
- 1309 —— Other coins, 23 and 16 groschen, (⅔ and ½ crowns); very fine. 3 pieces
- 1310 HANOVER. ⅔ crown of 1698, IN RECTO DECVS; nearly uncirculated.
- 1311 —— George V., thaler, very fine; Grand Duke Frederick, gulden and half do., very fine. 3 pieces
- 1312 BAVARIA. Ludwig I., 1828, fine medal crown (Zehn eine feine mark), with 9 royal portraits on reverse; rare.
- 1313 —— Max. II., two gulden (80 cents) and crown, with "Patrona Bavariae" standing on reverse; both very fine. 2 pieces
- 1314 —— Double gulden and gulden; fine. 2 pieces
- 1315 FRANKFORT. Double gulden, 1846, and thaler of 1863, with view of the City Hall; fine. 2 pieces
- 1316 —— Gulden of 1846, with 36 grote of Bremen; very fine. 2 pieces
- 1317 BADEN. Grand Duke Frederick, uncirculated thaler.
- 1318 ADOLPHUS FREDERICK, Bishop of Bamberg, fine and rare crown, 1761.
- 1319 FRANCIS I., Emperor, 1745, splendid crown; rev. "Augusta Vin Delissis," the Genius seated, holding a pine-apple; rare.
- 1320 JOHN FREDERICK, two-third crown; rev. EX DURIS GLORIA, 1675, palm on a rock grounded in the sea; fine and rare.
- 1321 —— Duplicate (⅔ crown), next year, 1676; also fine and rare.

Foreign Silver Coins.

1,50   1322 HENNEBERG dollar of 1692, hen crowned; in fair preservation; very rare.

10   1323 CARL FURST ZU ISENBURG, "12 kreuzer, 1811," and 12 and 20 kr., and other pieces resembling medalets of different ages and nationalities; some very fine and rare.   10 pieces

35   1324 MEDALET (¼ crown) of Basle, with a view of the city, and another, same size, equally fine; both rare.   2 pieces

75   1325 UNCLASSIFIED German coins of the XIVth and XVth Centuries, with others more modern; a selected, fine, and valuable lot; denarius or penny size.   12 pieces

5   {
1326 CRUSADERS silver and base pennies, with others of German and French origin; very rare lot.   12 pieces
1327 —— Similar lot.   14 pieces
1327* Similar coins, descending in the scale of antiquity and increasing in size.   20 pieces
1328 Repetition of last, old groat size, and base; many valuable coins.   10 pieces
}

10   1329 POLAND (of the last king), Frederick the Great, Leopold the 1st, etc., etc., slightly base; quarter-dollar size.   10 pieces

5   {
1330 Similar lot, unclassified, base.   10 pieces
1331 —— Twelve and six "Einen Thalers," etc., etc.   20 pieces
1332 —— Repetition of last.   20 pieces
1333 —— The same.   20 pieces
1334 —— Another, same.   20 pieces
1335 —— Same, reduced in size.   20 pieces
1336 —— Same as last.   20 pieces
1337 —— Same as last.   20 pieces
}

10   1338 —— Same; in this lot many old pennies.   20 pieces

5   1339 —— Closing lot, small base coins.   75 pieces

10   1340 FINE silver coins of Brunswick, Holland, Austria, etc.; average dime value.   6 pieces

10   1341 FINE uncirculated silver coins, 1 franc, 25 centimes, 6 kreutzers, etc.   6 pieces

7   1342 UNCLASSIFIED coins, weight 1 oz.

1 25   1343 ANHALT. Bear on a turreted wall, 1852; fine thaler.

45   1344 —— Twenty mark (half-dollar), 1809.

5   1345 —— Six einen thaler, uncirculated, 1861, and another, slightly circulated.   2 pieces

Switzerland.

20   1346 BERNE. Twenty kreutzer of 1656, bear walking, and double-headed eagle, same; rev. large B; rare.   2 pieces

Foreign Silver Coins. 61

12 1347 BERNE. Ten kr., 1756, 20 do., 1766; fine. 2 pieces
14 1348 ——— Five, two and a half, and one batzen; fine. 4 pieces
10 1349 BASLE. Three batze, 1809.
17c 1350 CHUR. Fine crown (X marck), 1794; rare.
2 30 1351 GENEVA REPUBLIC, 1723, crown, POST TENEBRAS LVX; scarce.
2 25 1352 ——— 1848, fine proof, 5 francs; rare.
1 2 1353 ——— Various types and values. 6 pieces
5 1354 GRAU-BUNDEN and FREYBURG. One batz. 2 pieces
11c 1355 LUCERN. Fine medal, half-dollar size, by *Schwendemann*, wild man to right and left of a shield, supporting a crown over the arms of the Canton; very fine and rare.
12 1356 ——— Five batzen, with same of cantons Vaud and Solure. 4 pieces
80 1357 ZURICH (Tigurinœ). Fine medal coin, half-dollar size, view of city.
20 1358 HELVETIA. Two francs, franc, and half do. 3 pieces

Denmark.

60 1359 FREDERICK II., 1539–1588. 1 MARCK, 1553; obv. title and arms (3 lions); rev. denomination and date; very fine and *extremely* rare.
3c 1360 CHRISTIAN IV., 1588–1648. Thick *dump*, 1611; obv. C 4, XII. (skilling); rev. arms (3 lions) crowned, very rare, with one of 8 sk., 1607, with his bust crowned. 2 pieces
50 1361 ——— Ducat, 1645, monogram as before, with the denomination II MARCK; rev. JUSTUS JUDEX and Hebrew letters, with half of the same piece XVI Sk.; both very fine, scarce. 2 pieces
65 1362 FREDERICK III., 1648–1670. Four marks (or two-thirds dollar) of 1652, cypher of his name under a crown; rev. arms of Denmark on a cross *potent*, DOMINVS PROVIDERIT; as fine as when struck and (this denomination) rare.
3c 1363 ——— Half of same, or two marks; on the reverse of this the lion of Norway is represented as standing on the curved handle of the battle-axe; as fine as last.
3 5 1364 ——— The half of last, one mark, or XVI sk., and equally fine.
1c 1365 FREDERICK III. Two skillings, various types; fine. 3 pieces

Foreign Silver Coins.

<small>4/6</small> 1366 CHRISTIAN V., 1670–1699. II MARCK, 1681, large C and 5 under a crown, PIETATE ET JVSTITIA; rev. similar to 1362; very fine, rare.

<small>/66</small> 1367 —— IIII marck (or two-third crown), 1693; obv. the royal monogram crowned and inclosed between two branches of laurel crossed, below two hammers crossed; rev. arms (3 lions) crowned and draped with the band and badge of the Elephant Order; very fine and rare.

<small>5 C</small> 1368 —— Half of same, or II marck, same date; equally fine and rare.

<small>45</small> 1369 —— IIII skilling, same type, and 8 sk.   2 pieces

<small>95</small> 1370 —— Mark, with his bust; rev. crown and motto, half do. or 16 sk. and 8 sk.; all uniform, making a fine set of   4 pieces

<small>85</small> 1371 FREDERICK IV., 1699–1730. Four marks (⅔ crown), 1725, same type as 1367, but varied in the motto and other particulars; equally fine, rare.

<small>/0</small> 1372 —— XVI skillings and 8 sk., with his bust; fine and ordinary; some used as buttons, the eyes now removed.   4 pieces

<small>/C</small> 1373 —— Repetition of last.   5 pieces

<small>4c</small> 1374 CHRISTIAN VI., 1730–1746. 24 skillings, 1731; obv. bust to the waist, wearing the band and badge of the Elephant Order; rev. arms of the three kingdoms (Norway, Sweden, and Denmark) on a cross *potent*, crowned; fine.   2 pieces

<small>25</small> 1375 —— 24 skilling; obv. the royal cypher crowned; rev. lion on a battle-axe, 1745; fine.   2 pieces

<small>/2</small> 1376 —— 8 skillings of this type, with one for his Province in America; rev. ship.   2 pieces

<small>30</small> 1377 FREDERICK V., 1746–1766. 24 skilling, two varieties, on both the royal cypher crowned; rev. of one similar to that of 1374, the other like 1375; fine.   2 pieces

<small>7c</small> 1378 CHRISTIAN VII., 1766–1808. Specie daler (for Holstein); obv. bust; rev. crowned shield, with the arms of Denmark, Norway, and Sweden, "1 — S P" at the sides, "60 Schilling Schlesw.-Holst. Courant, 17–95"; fair, scarce.

<small>8c</small> 1379 —— Same, except legend, which is "1 Rigs Daler Species," 1797; very fine and rare.

<small>/C</small> 1380 —— One-fourth rigsdaler courant; obv. the royal monogram crowned, "5 STYKER 1 RIGSDALER SPECIES"; rev. * 4 * STYKER RIGSDALER COURANT, the date 1803, two hammers crossed and the initials J. G. M.; an uncommon coin, in fine preservation, with 4 smaller pieces of same king.   5 pieces

Foreign Silver Coins. 63

100 1381 CHRISTIAN VIII., 1842. One rigsbank daler, "30 schill. courant" (55 cents), undraped bust; rev. a crowned shield quartered, bearing the arms of the three kingdoms, with those of Holstein, Gothen, and Warden, the whole decorated with the band of the Elephant Order, etc. ; fine.

40 1382 FREDERICK VII., 1863. Piece of the same value as last, with its half; both fine. 2 pieces

10 1383 —— Ten cents for the Danish West India Islands and others, unclassified. 4 pieces

Sweden.

200 1384 GUSTAVUS I. (VASA), 1523-1560. Obv. bearded, crowned, and mailed bust of the king, with sword and globe, GOSTAVS D. G. REX SVVECIE ; rev. three coats-of-arms crowned, 15-60, BEATVS, QVI, TIMET, DOMINVM ; in excellent preservation, and very rare half-crown.

120 1385 CHARLES XI., 1660-1697. Four marks (⅔ crown) of 1672, fine bust in wig and royally draped ; rev. a shield charged with three crowns, under a crown 4—M. DOMINVS PROTECTOR MEVS ; extremely fine and rare.

10 1386 CHARLES XI., 1660-1697. Two fine little coins, dated 1667 and 1668, both with the royal cypher and three crowns. 2 pieces

7 1387 CHARLES XII., 1697-1718. Two small coins, representing his first and last year ; almost exactly like those of his predecessor. 2 pieces

60 1388 ULRICA-ELEONORA, Queen, 1719. One mark of this date, with her bust ; fine and *very* rare.

25 1389 FREDERICK IX., 1720-1751. 10 Or., 1740, letter F placed in pairs back to back, so as to form a cross ; rev. three crowns ; very fine coin, quarter-dollar size.

20 1390 GUSTAVUS III., 1771-1792. ⅓ rigsdaler and ⅙ rigsdaler, 1779 and 1796, and another; fine. 3 pieces

25 1391 GUSTAVUS ADOLPHUS, 1792-1809. Fine bust of the "Lion of the North" on a coin (⅙ rigs dal.) of 1805 ; uncirculated and *rare*.

25 1392 CHARLES XIII., 1809-1818. 1/24 rigs daler, 1814 ; uncirculated.

52 1393 CHARLES XIV. 60 skillings (½ specie dollar), 1819, very fine, with one of Frederick VI. of Denmark, same value. 2 pieces

8 1394 —— 8 skillings, 24 skillig, ⅛ rigs specie daler, etc. ; fine lot of coins, weight 2 oz.

Foreign Silver Coins.

1395 OSCAR, 1846. ½ specie dollar, nearly proof; this has the lion of Norway holding the battle-axe in his paws, not as formerly, standing on its handle; a very beautiful coin.
1396 —— Set of coins from 24 sk. to 25 ore. 3 pieces
1397 —— Half and quarter-dollar, fine. 2 pieces
1398 CHARLES XV., 1861. Nearly proof crown, with lion erect, holding battle-axe; rare.
1399 —— 24 skilling (⅛), same type, and 12 sk.; nearly proof. 2 pieces

Russia.

1400 SERIES. 25, 20, 15, 10, 5 kopecs; all uncirculated and brilliant. 8 pieces
1401 Two old coins, one without date. 2 pieces

Turkey.

1402 DOLLAR of fine silver, do. of Tunis? (nearly pure), two rupees and one do.; all good silver; weight 2½ oz. av. 4 pieces
1403 COLLECTION of various sizes and quality, from fine to base; none poor. 2½ oz.

Spain and South America.

1404 PHILIP IIII., 1632. Half-dollar for Holland; rare.
1405 PHILIP V. Various pistareens, some of Charles II. and III. 6 pieces
1406 CHARLES III. and FERDINAND VI. Pistareens and half do., 2 of each. 4 pieces
1407 CHARLES III., 1772. Dollar, very fine.
1408 —— Quarter, nearly uncirculated, and ⅛ do. 2 pieces
1409 CHARLES IIII. Dollar, half do., quarter do.; all fine. 3 pieces
1410 FERDINAND VII. Dollar (5 pesetas) of Catalonia, 1802; very fine and rare.
1411 —— Small coins, with others, ¼ and ⅛ths and ¹⁄₁₆ths, over an ounce in weight; the lot.
1412 ISABELLA II. Beautiful, nearly uncirculated, set—dollar, half, quarter, eighth, and sixteenth. 5 pieces
1413 MEXICO. Dollar of August 1, 1822; fine, scarce.
1414 —— Republic of 1860, very fine dollar.
1415 —— Quarter and eighth do., 1846; very fine. 2 pieces
1416 —— Maximilian dollar of 1866; very fine.

Ancient Coins.

300 — 1417 PERU. ~~Beautiful dollar~~ of Echenique, 1832; rare.
105 — 1418 —— Same of the Republic, 1830; uncirculated, rare.
112 — 1419 BOLIVIA. Dollar of the "Liberator," 1834; very fine.
32 — 1420 —— Half and quarter do. 2 pieces
100 — 1421 BRAZIL. Dollar (2,000 reis), 1857; fine.
28 — 1422 —— Half same, ¼ do., and ⅛ do.; fine. 3 pieces
50 — 1423 CHILI. Half-dollar, same of South Peru. 2 pieces
70 — 1424 —— 2 reals, quarter-doll., with others same value; fine lot; quartz. 10 pieces
16 — 1425 SOUTH AMERICAN reals, etc.; great variety. 10 pieces
11 — 1426 FAUSTIN I., HAYTI. 3 base coins, with "50 Pennia" of Roumania, etc. 7 pieces
60 — 1427 ENGLAND, BRUNSWICK, and LUNENBERG. Sixpence of Anna, small coins of Victoria, etc.; ½ oz.; the lot.
12 — 1428 —— Marien groschen of Br. and L., average dime value. 8 pieces
2,50 — 1429 SCUDO of the City of Bologna in Italy; obv. shield, with the arms quartered, LIBERTAS in second and third quarters, in ex. 10 P(auls), 1797; rev. Madonna and Child on a cloud above the city, value $1.13; fine and scarce.
7 — 1430 BASE silver coins, unclassified; pretty lot. 15 pieces
3 — 1431 —— Indifferent lot. 50 pieces

ANCIENT COINS.

Silver.

50 — 1432 ATHENS. Drachma of the early type, a sharp, well-preserved coin, completely covered with oxidation.
70 — 1433 ALEXANDER. Drachma; rev. Jupiter, and one very fine; rev. Pegassus. 2 pieces
53 — 1434 BARBAROUS and unknown rude head; rev. horseman, with shield; drachma.
1,71 — 1435 —— Head of Ceres; rev. Venus and Cupid, ins. in Greek, DIOS EXO; didrachm, well executed and preserved; very *curious*.
95 — 1436 HYLEA. Head of Minerva; rev. lion springing on the back of a stag; didrachm; fair, rare.
52 — 1437 ROME. Double denarius for the Campania; very fine.
35 — 1438 JULIA GENS; rev. CAESAR, Æneas with his father and the Palladium, Marcus Gens, Cordia Gens, etc.; fair lot denarii.

5

23 1439 HADRIAN, Ant. Pius, Faustina (mother), and M. Aurelius; very good denarii. 4 pieces
15 1440 GETA, Maximinus, Gallien, etc.; billon. 8 pieces

Bronze.

GREEK.

11 1441 AGRAGENTUM, Bruttium, Brundusium, Cales, Tarentum, and other Italian Provinces; a very interesting lot, from fair to fine; 1st to 3d size. 12 pieces
10 1442 CORINTH, Thurium, Mamertini, Metapontum, and others Italia; generally poor, but uncommon. 12 pieces
6 1443 ARCADIA, Siciyon, Carthage, Syracuse, etc., autonomous and regal; fair to poor. 12 pieces
10 1444 RHEGIUM, Thurium, Cales, Opuntum, etc.; 1st to 3d size; a carefully selected and valuable lot. 12 pieces
17 1445 SYRACUSE, Tauromenium, Campania, etc., etc.; another valuable lot. 12 pieces
11 1446 HIERO II., Ptolemy I., Velia, Athens, Argos, etc. 12 pieces
10 1447 CAMPANIA, Maronea, Populonia, Corinth, etc., etc.; small and poor. 12 pieces
11 1448 ATHENS, Crotona, Cumaea, Argos, etc., etc.; poor. 12 pieces
15 1449 CALYMNA, Thurium, Tauromenium, Carthage, Corinth, etc., etc.; good lot, selected. 12 pieces
5 5 1450 PTOLEMY I. Large brass, head of Jupiter; rev. eagle on thunderbolt; fine. 2 pieces
6 1451 UNCLASSIFIED Greek coins, small. 20 pieces

Roman Brass Coins.

20 1452 As, Janus head; rev. prow. Size 22; very good.
15 1453 —— Varieties of same; fair. 3 pieces
5 1454 VALERIA GENS. Head of Venus; rev. Minerva, etc.; one, rev. star, and others; fair to poor; various sizes. 10 pieces
15 1455 AUGUSTUS, Trib. Pol. XXXIIII., well patinated, and his son-in-law, Agrippa, also patinated; good coins. 2 pieces
15 1456 —— Varieties of Augustus; Augustus and Agrippa for Nemauses, and Agrippa; a good lot, without duplicates. 10 pieces
12 1457 —— Others of Augustus and Agrippa; indifferent. 10 pieces

Ancient Coins.   67

15   1458 TIBERIUS. Rev. globe and rudder, and one, rev. altar; 2d size (two fine).   3 pieces

10   1459 GERMANICUS, Drusus, and Antonia, wife of Drusus; rare coins, in very fair preservation; 2d size.   3 pieces

12   1460 CALIGULA and Claudius; 2d size; very good.   5 pieces

25   1461 CLAUDIUS. Laureated head; rev. Hope standing; first bronze, in good preservation, the obverse being fine and very rare.

15   1462 NERO. Rev. the Genius standing and Victory walking; 2d size; fair. With one of LIVIA; rev. SALVS AVGVSTA; fair and very rare.   7 pieces

20   1463 GALBA. Rev. LIBERTAS, Liberty standing. 2d size; sharp and fairly patinated, rare.

15   1464 —— Another, different reverse, with others of the second size of Vespasian and Titus; very good lot, 2d size.   4 pieces

5   1465 DOMITIAN. 1st and 2d size; fine to poor.   12 pieces

25   1466 —— 1st size; rev. IOVI VICTORI S. C., Jupiter seated holding Victory and hasta; fine and rare.

7½   ⎧ 1467 NERVA. Second size; rev. Fortune standing; very good. With Trajan, same size; ordinary.   6 pieces
    ⎨ 1468 TRAJAN. 2d size; rev. Victory crowning the Emperor, and others of Hadrian; fine lot.   6 pieces
    ⎩ 1469 —— 1st and 2d size; rather poor.   6 pieces

45   1469* HADRIAN. 1st brass; rev. Rome seated, holding the hand of the Emperor, standing; a scarce type, in excellent preservation.

    ⎧ 1470 —— 2d size; various reverses, some rare.   6 pieces
    ⎪ 1471 —— 1st and 2d size; indifferent.   12 pieces
5   ⎨ 1472 AELIUS and Ant. Pius. 2d size; good lot (several rare reverses).   12 pieces
    ⎪ 1473 ANTONINUS PIUS. 1st size.   5 pieces
    ⎩ 1474 —— Various, indifferent; and Faustina.   6 pieces

7½   1475 FAUSTINA. 1st and 2d, two sizes; good to fair.   5 pieces

5   1476 —— Similar; ordinary.   8 pieces

5   1477 MARCUS AURELIUS. 1st and 2d size; fair.   6 pieces

12   1478 —— With rare reverses, and others, unclassified; valuable lot.   4 pieces

10   1479 LUCIUS VERUS and Lucilla (wife). No duplicates; 1st and 2d size; good.   4 pieces

12   1480 SEPTIMUS SEVERUS, Crispina (wife of Commodus), and Julia Maesa; 1st and 2d brass, fair.   3 pieces

7 2   1481 ALEXANDER SEVERUS and Julia Mamaea; 1st brass, fair.   2 pieces

68   *Modern Copper Coins.*

5   1482 MAXIMINUS, Caracalla, and others, earlier; 1st and 2d size; rather poor.   8 pieces
15 1483 MAXIMINUS I. and Gordian III. Patinated and *very fine*; 1st brass; desirable.   2 pieces
11 1484 —— Repetition of last; fine.   2 pieces
16 1485 —— Same; very good.   6 pieces
1/2 1486 PHILIP (senior), Gordian III., and others; 1st size.   6 pieces
      1487 OTACILIA SEVERA, and others; 1st and 2d size; fair.   6 pieces
      1488 TREBONIANUS GALLUS, Alexander, Volusianus, etc.; 1st brass; some rare and fine.   6 pieces
10 1489 VALERIAN I. Very good and rare; 1st size.
8   1490 UNCLASSIFIED Roman Imperial coins of fair character; a mass containing duplicates of the preceding series, with the small brass of succeeding emperors to the Byzantine period.   50 pieces
3   1491 —— Similar; poorer.   100 pieces
3   1492 —— Similar.   67 pieces
25 1493 JOHANNES I. (Zimices). Coins, with the effigies of Jesus Christ nimbused and with the title of King of kings; both large and second size; fair.   4 pieces
12 1494 ANASTASIUS I. Large brass, and other Byzantine; rare lot.   5 pieces
15 1495 LEO? Cup-shape coin, etc.   8 pieces

MODERN COPPER COINS.

(Since Eighth Century.)

2c 1495* CUFIC coins, with figures of animals, and inscription in the character that preceded the Arabic; very rare and interesting, with one Byzantine.   3 pieces
20c 1496 ROGER I., Count of Sicily. A Crusader, A.D. 1072–1101; obv. Roger in mail, cap-a-pie, mounted on a caparisoned horse, ROGE–RIVS COMES; rev. Madonna and Jesus; very rare.   Size 17
      [Much the best example that I have seen.]
12 1497 ARABIC, Cufic, and Assamese; desirable lot.   6 pieces
10 1498 THICK coins of various nationalities; old.   10 pieces
10 1499 FRENCH coppers; liards of the early Barons and Dukes, *e. g.*, Godfrey of Bouillon, Mont-Beiliard, Charles X. (Mantua), Leopold I., etc., etc.; in fine preservation.   18 pieces

Modern Copper Coins.

6	1500	FRENCH coppers; Liards of Kings of France, of Maria, Duchess of Montpensier, etc., etc.	20 pieces
3	1501	—— Similar lot.	20 pieces
4	1502	—— Similar to last.	20 pieces
5	1503	—— Same.	50 pieces
10	1504	—— Another similar lot.	40 pieces
8	1505	—— Similar.	40 pieces
8	1506	—— Similar.	40 pieces
9	1507	—— Similar.	40 pieces
10	1508	—— Unclassified, larger size, and very fine, from Louis XVI.	10 pieces
5	1509	—— Similar; not as fine.	10 pieces
5	1510	—— Miscellaneous and new.	20 pieces
3	1511	—— Similar to last.	20 pieces
3	1512	—— Same.	20 pieces
4	1513	—— Same as last.	20 pieces
3	1514	—— Same.	20 pieces
4	1515	SPANISH coppers, in good preservation.	10 pieces
5	1516	—— Similar lot. " "	10 pieces
4	1517	—— Miscellaneous, some of France.	15 pieces
4	1518	—— Similar to last.	15 pieces
4	1519	PORTUGAL. Large and fine.	10 pieces
5	1520	Same and Brazil.	20 pieces
	1521	Similar to last.	20 pieces
	1522	Similar; more mixed.	20 pieces
	1523	Another similar lot.	20 pieces
4	1524	MEXICAN, and other Spanish and French colonies, etc.	20 pieces
	1525	MISCELLANEOUS coppers.	20 pieces
	1526	Similar lot.	20 pieces
	1527	Same.	20 pieces
	1528	Same.	20 pieces
	1529	Same.	20 pieces
6	1530	The same; selected and fine.	20 pieces
7	1531	Similar; equally fine.	20 pieces
12	1532	ITALY. Pius VI., VII., and IX., and Gregory XVI.; large and fine.	5 pieces
10	1533	—— 5, 3, 2, 1, and mezzo baiocchi; good set.	5 pieces
17	1534	—— Pius IV., with his bust, an uncirculated set of 4, 2, and 1 soldi; scarce.	3 pieces
7	1535	—— Three baiocchi of the Republic of '49; bright, scarce, and others, fine.	5 pieces

Modern Copper Coins.

1536 SWEDEN. Plate of pure copper, bearing a stamp in each corner and in the centre; value "½ Daler," gold, date 1715, time of Charles XII. (with the monogram of that King), size 4 x 4 inches; *rare*.

1537 —— Frederick IX. Piece of copper as above; same dimensions, but of double *thickness*; value "1 Daler," date 1745 (cypher of the King); equally fine and rare.

1538 —— Christina. Large copper (size 30), 1639; fine and scarce.

1539 —— Charles XI., 1680. Similar; same size; very fine.

1540 —— A number of these large and scarce coins, some half of the value and size of last; Christina, Gustavus Adolphus, etc.; valuable lot.   8 pieces

1541 —— Old coppers, Charles XII., etc. (one of Baron Goerck's Dalers).   12 pieces

1542 —— Similar; unclassified.   12 pieces
1543 —— Similar; unclassified.   12 pieces
1544 —— Another lot; same.   12 pieces
1545 —— Same.   12 pieces
1546 —— Same; small coins.   20 pieces
1547 —— Same as last.   20 pieces
1548 —— Closing lot; mixed.   24 pieces

1549 RUSSIA. Large thick coppers, value 5 kopecs, engrailed edges; no duplicates.   5 pieces

1550 —— Similar, with others half size of last.   5 pieces

1551 —— Similar to 1549 (5 kopecs), with plain edges.   5 pieces

1552 —— Same, with 3 and 2 kopecs.   5 pieces
1553 —— Miscellaneous; all sizes.   10 pieces
1554 —— Similar.   15 pieces
1555 —— Same.   15 pieces

1556 SWITZERLAND. Thin base coins of the Cantons.   20 pieces
1557 —— Similar.   20 pieces
1558 —— Same.   20 pieces

1559 GREECE. 10, 5, and 1 lepta; very good condition.   3 pieces

1560 —— 10 and 5 lepta; varieties.   5 pieces

1561 GERMANY, Austria, Poland, and Hungary. Fine.   10 pieces

1562 —— Unclassified; very fine.   20 pieces
1563 —— Similar; equally fine.   20 pieces
1564 —— Same; very fine.   20 pieces

Coin Catalogues.

3	1565	DENMARK, Sweden, Russia, etc.; fine.	20 pieces
3	1566	HOLLAND, etc.; good lot.	20 pieces
40	1567	FRANCE. 10 centimes of the Republic of '48; *proof*, rare.	
5	1568	—— A selection; bright and uncirculated.	14 pieces
10	1569	TURKEY and Arabia.	12 pieces
8	1570	SUMATRA, Liberia, etc.; fine lot.	25 pieces
5	1571	SICILY and Italy (in general).	10 pieces
3	1572	—— Same.	10 pieces
3	1573	ENGLAND and Ireland.	15 pieces
1	1574	—— Same; poor.	15 pieces
2	1575	CANADA; fair.	20 pieces
10	1576	—— Same; fair.	20 pieces
25	1577	JAPAN. Oval and round; large size (Tempo's).	3 pieces
2	1578	CHINA. Cash.	43 pieces
7	1579	SELECTED coins of interest; all in good and fine condition, some square and thin.	75 pieces
8	1580	TOKENS used by the English and issued by their tradesmen in the 18th Century, penny and half-penny size; ordinary. With a mixture of other English.	75 pieces
3	1581	—— More mixed, many French, etc.	75 pieces
2	1582	OLD coppers; miscellaneous.	300 pieces
	1583	Similar.	300 pieces
	1584	Another; same.	300 pieces
	1585	Similar lot.	300 pieces
	1586	COPPERS of the twopenny, penny, halfpenny, and smaller size.	200 pieces

COIN CATALOGUES.

30 1587 HARRISON SANDFORD. By Edward Cogan. Sold by Bangs, Merwin & Co., 27 Nov., 1874. Priced.

15 1588 PRIVATE SALE by Butler & Durrie, Madison, Wis., 1874.

30 1589 PRIVATE COLLECTION, by J. W. Haseltine. Sold by the Messrs. Leavitt, January, 1875. Priced.

25 1590 Duplicate copy. Also priced.

25 1591 PRIVATE COLLECTION, by J. W. Haseltine. Sold by Thomas Birch & Son, Philadelphia, Dec., 1875.

1,25 1592 M. J. COHEN. Edward Cogan. Sold by Bangs, Merwin & Co., Oct., 1875. Priced.

100 1593 Duplicate. Also priced.

50 1594 Duplicate. Priced.

1595 EDWARD COGAN. May, 1875, and one June, same year; both priced. 2 pieces
1596 —— Duplicate of June sale, and another same year; both priced. 2 pieces
1597 J. E. GAY. By W. H. Strobridge, April, 1875. Priced.
1598 GEO. STENZ. By W. H. Strobridge. Sold by G. A. Leavitt & Co., May, 1875. Priced.
1599 Duplicate. Also priced.
1600 JAMES H. TAYLOR. By W. H. Strobridge. Sold by G. A. Leavitt & Co., Nov., 1875 (3 priced). 4 copies

END OF PART II.

Addenda. 73

ADDENDA TO PART II.

1601 GUINEA. (Spade-shape shield.) Geo. III., 1794; fine, scarce.
1602 DUCAT, Belgium. PAVAE CRESCVNT, etc., 1818; fine.
1603 EIGHTH-DOUBLOON ($2) Republic Colombia, 1832; fine.
1604 CAROLINA dollar of A. Bechtler (27 gs.); fine.
1605 PATTERN Gobrecht dollar, 1836, U. S. Mint; tarnished and slightly circulated, but fine and scarce.
1606 UNITED STATES cent, 1794; circulated, but fine. Massachusetts do., and New Jersey cent.   3 pieces
1607 CENT of 1799; undoubtedly false, but unique in the manner of making it so; a curiosity.
1608 TEMPO, AUSTRALIAN card, English two-pence, melanotypes, cards, medalets, and coppers; several pieces rare.   52 pieces
1609 ANCIENT Egyptian coin of *Ptolemaou Basileou* (Greek), of a fabric quite unique; obv. female head in elephant-skin hood; rev. eagle displayed, mark remains of ancient lathe-work; second size, bronze.
1610 ANCIENT Indian coin, with sacred bull and leopard, Cufic ins.; other Bactrian, Greek Imperial, and Roman coins, in fine preservation, and several of much interest and very rare.   10 pieces
1611 COIN of Nepaul (India), and other Oriental and ancient coppers; fine to poor.   12 pieces
1612 TICAL (60 cts.), Siam. Tenth yen of Japan; itzbu in silver and same in gold.   4 pieces
1613 BROKEN silver, used in Canton for change, and other European-Asiatic silver coins of about the value of 10 cents each, some same value unclassified; all very fine.   13 pieces
1614 MODERN Greek drachma, lira, and quarter-dollar. 3 pieces
1615 MICELLANEOUS coppers; fine.   22 pieces
1616 ANCIENT Roman copper coins, the collection of an amateur, in wrappers; generally patinated and well preserved.   57 pieces
1617 PENNY of Henry III., England; fine.

Addenda.

1618 SIX-PENCE and three-pence of Queen Elizabeth (England), 1561; uncirculated. 2 pieces

1619 SHILLING of Queen Anna, 1708; ex. fine.

1620 PATTERN copper farthings of William and Mary, and Mary II.; on the former a bust of each on opposite sides; on the latter her bust, with a rose-tree on the reverse with the motto CANDORE DECVS; this is very fine; the other much corroded; both *rare*. 2 pieces

1621 HALF-PENNY and farthing of William and Mary, and same of William III.; three of the pieces in very good preservation. 4 pieces

1622 FARTHINGS of Charles I., and half-penny and farthing (CAROLVS A CAROLO) of Charles II.; very good lot. 5 pieces

1623 "HIBERNIA" of James II., "VOCE POPULI," and farthings of Geo. I. and II.; good lot. 4 pieces

1624 CROWN of Leopold I. (Germany), 1695; very fine.

1625 DOLLAR of Gen. Vargas (Spain); good example, rare.

1626 Same of Ferd. VII., thaler of Fred. William, and 5 lire of Napoleon, 1808. 3 pieces

1627 "LIBERTAS AMERICANA" and "Funeral" medalet of Gen'l Washington; the first in copper, with white plating; the other tin; poor. 2 pieces

1628 "WOOD" half-penny, shin-plasters, etc., etc.; in the lot, several good politicals. 66 pieces

1629 GROAT of Edward III.; pierced.

1630 SHILLING of Charles I. *Mint-mark* F, the letter placed horizontally above the crown; the head and arms within circle of pearls; *extremely* fine and rare type.

1631 SHILLING of same, without *inner* circle; stained, but fine and rare.

1632 SIX-PENCE of Elizabeth, and same of Anna. 2 pieces

1633 SHILLINGS of George II. (old head and young do.) and George III., 1787. 3 pieces

1634 REALS of Mexico and Central America; *fine*. 3 pieces

1635 WOOD'S Minstrels token; uncirculated, silver.

1636 HALF-DIME of 1800 (U. S. Mint); fair, scarce.

1637 CROWN of Louis XVI. (France); fair, scarce.

1638 THREE and one cents, Feuchtwanger's composition, French medal (Louis Nap. Bonaparte), Nassau Water Works, antique Greek coins, and united cent of 1801. 10 pieces

Addenda. 75

9c 1639 LARGE bronze of Ptolemy I., head of Jupiter; rev. eagle, with folded wings; another, with wings *raised*, a cornucopiæ counter-sunk (or incused) on one wing; fine. Size 26. 2 pieces
12 1640 Same, with smaller. 4 pieces
1c 1641 GREEK imperial, struck at Alexandria. 30 pieces
1c 1642 ROMAN imperial of the lower Empire; fine. 50 pieces
9   1643 —— Similar lot. 100 pieces
c   1644 —— Same. 165 pieces
c   1645 TURKISH coins of base silver, and unclassified copper and nickel coins. 33 pieces

Colonial Coppers.

13.25 1646 A RARE token or *sous* of Louis XV. Obv. bust; rev. native Indian standing, with his arms (bow and quiver of arrows); behind him a grove of trees and log-fence, COL FRANC DE L'AM, 1751; obv. fine, rev. fair. Size 19
15 1647 NOVA-CONSTELATIO and Constellatio; one very fine; varieties. 3 pieces
15 1648 NOVA-CÆSAREA, 1788; a variety, on which the first figure 8 in the date is quite above the line, touching the base of the plough; in fine condition, very rare. With others of 1787, on large planchets; good lot. 4 pieces
5   1649 —— Various dates and varieties; ordinary. 12 pieces
1c 1650 "AUCTORI-VERMON" and "Vermontensium"; varieties; rare, rather poor. 6 pieces
4c 1651 —— "Baby-head" to r., and a rare variety, with head to l., 1786; better than usually found.
10 1652 AUCTORI-CONNEC., with head to l.; others to r., mailed busts and draped do.; from poor to fine; a good *lot*. 14 pieces
1c 1653 WASHINGTON token of 1783; Mott's do.; Talbot, Allum & Lee do.; North American do.; Wood do.; and Franklin cents; from poor to fine; a good lot. 10 pieces
12 1654 WASHINGTON cent of 1782, Higby do.; both poor and false.
15 1655 WASHINGTON medal, known as one of the "Season" series second Presidency; cow and calf; battered and very poor, rare.
53 1656 BOLENS, "Inimica Tyrannis"; very fair.

76 *Addenda.*

United States Cents.

5.00	1657	1793, chain, dot after the word *Liberty;* dark, but *good* impression; *rare*.
6.75	1658	1793, wreath, treefoil upright; *very* fine, rare.
5.5	1659	1793, one of both varieties; very poor. 2 pieces
3.0	1660	1794, varieties (one cleaned); ordinary. 2 pieces
1.50	1661	1795, plain edge; fine.
1.75	1662	1796, Liberty Cap, fine impression, but little circulated; very dark, rare.
4.5	1663	1797, 1798, and 1799; the last altered (the '98 fine). 3 pieces
1.c	1664	1800, fine, dark (—); and 1801, fine, but cleaned. 2 pieces
8c	1665	1802, fine, dark (—); and 1803, nearly uncirculated. 2 pieces
2.55	1666	1804; very poor, rare.
2.5	1667	1805, 1806, and 1807; fair and poor. 3 pieces
4c	1668	1808; a good cent, but dark.
6.50	1669	1809; *extremely* fine; color dark, almost black, but highly desirable and rare.
6.0	1670	1811 and 1812; very fair. 2 pieces
1.50	1671	1813; as sharp and full as when struck; very slightly corroded, but desirable.
2.5	1672	1814 and 1816 (broken die), the latter bright; both fine. 2 pieces
2.5	1673	1820; uncirculated and brilliant. 2 pieces
3.0	1674	1827; very fine, but little circulated.
6	1675	Cents and half-cents, unclassified; a continuation of the series, with duplicates of some of the foregoing dates, with the exception of the nickel and small copper, which are very fine; generally poor. 71 pieces

United States Silver Coins.

1.75	1676	Dollar of 1795. Extremely fine; nearly uncirculated.
8c	1677	Half-dollar, 1795; ordinary.
4.75	1678	Half-dime, 1797, *uncirculated;* not brilliant, but entirely *perfect*; in this condition *very* rare.
10	1679	Dimes of 1820, 1834, and 1873; all fine. 3 pieces
5.5	1680	Half-dollar of 1873, rare, and one of 1871. 2 pieces
3.c	1681	Twenty cents of 1875; brilliant, scarce. 3 pieces

Addenda. 77

1682 TRADE DOLLAR of 1873, and dollar of the Republic of Mexico, 1870; both very fine. 2 pieces

1683 TRADE DOLLAR of 1873; brilliant proof, rare.

1684 PATTERN "V," "III," and "I" nickel cents, 1868; diademed head of Liberty on obverse; beautiful proof. 3 pieces

1685 PATTERN "50," "25," "10" cents of 1869; head of Liberty, with Phrygian bonnet; brilliant proofs, rare. 3 pieces

1686 Same, with diademed head. 3 pieces

1687 Same, with filleted head and star. 3 pieces

1688 PROOF SET of 1857 (7 pieces), *untarnished;* seldom found in this beautiful condition; very rare.

1689 Same of 1862. (7 pieces.)

1690 Same of 1863. (7 pieces.)

1691 Same of 1864. (9 pieces.)

1692 Same of 1865. (9 pieces.)

1693 Same of 1866. (9 pieces.)

1694 Same of 1867. (10 pieces.)

1695 Same of 1868. (10 pieces.)

1696 Same of 1871. (10 pieces.)

1697 Same of 1873; very rare. (10 pieces.)

1698 Same; another of 1873; very rare. (10 pieces.)

1699 Same of 1874. (7 pieces.)

1700 Same of 1875. (7 pieces.)

1701 Same; duplicate set of this date.

1702 Same of 1876. (8 pieces.)

1703 Same; duplicate set of this date.

1704 FINE gold dollar of Carolus III. of Spain, two uncirculated half dollars from California mint, and two octagon quarters. 5 pieces

1705 BROOKLYN City badge, presented in 1866 "To one of its veterans." It has on side, a female standing, holding the old Roman *Fasces*, a symbol of Liberty; on the other, a soldier on guard; prettily designed, and struck in copper; suspended by a bar and red velvet ribbon. It has a companion representing instead of the soldier, a veteran *sailor*, with these, two Confederate buttons. 4 pieces

1706 BRONZE PLACQUE. Representing "Cornwallis Resigning his Sword to Washington." Executed in bas-relief, and finished in a careful manner, very rare. 4x6 inches

78   *Addenda.*

1707 BUST OF CALVIN. (A shell, head side only), and miscellaneous coll. of copper and minute silver tokens, several politicals and rare cards.   67 pieces

1708 CONFEDERATE PAPERS, Furloughs, Receipts, etc. With a bundle of Bank and Treasury Notes, from 1 to 100 dollars.   100 pieces

1709 —— Bond or Certificate for $5,000, and Bank Notes for sums ranging from, and including 500 dollars to 10 cents ; many rare.   100 pieces

1710 —— Bank Notes from 500 to 2 dollars.   100 pieces

1711 —— Uncounted, from 500 to 5 dollars, with a rare Virginia Continental and Congressional Note. Old manuscripts, etc., etc. The lot.

1712 BUNDLE of Coin Catalogues.   50 pieces

1713 —— Others with pamphlets relating to coins.   20 pieces

1714 —— Large paper, priced, illustrated, etc.   12 pieces

1715 RARE CATALOGUES, priced, do., illustrated, do. ; among them H. H. Leeds & Co., Nov. 21, 1863; Louis Borg, 1867; Mackenzie, 1869; Mickley, priced. Clay, priced and illustrated, etc.   9 pieces

1716 OLD BRONZE French Medals ; a number selected from several hundreds, for superiority of workmanship and fine preservation. Among them, Henry II. and Henry IV., Louis XIII. and his Queen, Mary de Medicis; Anna (of Austria); Charles IX. and his Queen ; Card. Richelieu; Francis II., with the title of King of France and Scotland. Contemporary, and very rare ; from size 24 to 36.   12 pieces

1717 Another selected lot. "Carolus Decimus," Maria de Medicis; Michael Angelo ; Anna (of Austria); Card. Mazarin; Louis XIV., and Maria Antoinette ; etc., etc. ; from fine to fair ; all uncommon.   20 pieces

1718 MEDALS OF LOUIS XIV. A great variety of reverses ; many superb pieces, but they are stained from passing through fire ; from size 24 to 48.   20 pieces

1719 —— Of Louis XIII., XIV., XV. and XVI. ; damaged.   20 pieces

1720 —— Napoleon I., etc. ; damaged.   40 pieces

1721 —— American and miscellaneous ; damaged.   50 pieces

1722 —— Gen'l Grant (*by Bovy*), fine and rare.

1723 —— Unclassified.   60 pieces

1724 SILVER TECAL of Siam, bullet shape and modern.   2 pieces

1725 —— Various.   12 pieces

Addenda. 79

1726 SCUDO of Tuscany. Odoardus Farnese, G. Duke, 1629. Uncirculated, very rare.
1727 CROWN and HALF CROWN of Peter 1st. (the Great) of Russia, nearly uncirculated, very rare. 2 pieces
1728 Same of Peter II., 1727 (son of Alexis), of Russia; rev. the Greek letter P arranged as a cross, by placing it at right angles with itself four times; very fine and rare.
1729 Same of Catherine I., equally fine and rare.
1730 Same of Anna (Ivanovne), 1731, uncirculated and very rare Crown.
1731 Same of John III. (Antonovitch), equally fine and rare Crown.
1732 CROWN and HALF CROWN of Elizabeth I. (Petrovna); extra fine. 2 pieces
1733 PETER III. (Feodorovitch), uncirculated Crown, 1762, very rare.
1734 SIGISMUND I., King of Poland. Silver coins, Groat and Half Groat size, 1506-1548; very fine. 5 pieces
1735 Same of Sigismund II., 1566-1569. 5 pieces
1736 Same of Stephen Bathori, 1575-1586. 3 pieces
1737 WLADISLAUS IIII., Poland, 1632-1648; splendid uncirculated Crown, 1637, very rare.
1738 AUGUSTUS III. (last King of Poland), 2-3 Crown of 1736; uncirculated, very rare.
1739 ALEXANDER I. (Kaiser of Poland), Crown, 1823; 10 Zlot; fine and rare.
1740 —— 5 Zlot and 2 Zlot, uncirculated. 2 pieces
1741 THALER OF CHRISTIAN V., 1603, Denmark; fine.
1742 HALF CROWN of Gustavus Vasa (Sweden), 1541, and 2 Marck (Half Thaler) of Charles XII., 1762; good pieces and very rare. 2 pieces
1743 SIGISMUND BATHORI, Prince of Transylvania, 1581-1598; obv. his body to the hips, head bare; rev. arms (claws of a bear) on a shield with angels supporting; splendid crown, very rare. (Wellenheim, 1387).
1744 COLLECTION of old and uncommon small silver Coins, such as Wladislam II. of Austria (1471), Charles I. of France and Roman Empress. 7 pieces
1745 DENARII of Hadrian and Sabina, many fine and rare reverses. 10 pieces
1746 LOT of Roman and Egyptian brass Coins of all sizes. 55 pieces
1747 —— Another more rare, including a very good first bronze of Claudius. 14 pieces

1748 SUPERB bronze Medal from Virginia to Winfield Scott. By *C. C. Wright*. Size 58
1749 HALF EAGLE, 1795, fine and scarce.
1750 CROWN OF GEORGE III., from Pistrucci's dies, nearly proof, rare.
1751 BIRTH MEDALET of the Count de Paris, 24 Augt., 1838, and small English Medalets of the Royal Children; rare lot. 12 pieces
1752 SILVER HALF DOLLAR (500 Reis) of Portugal, Half Tecal (30 cts.) of Siam, and Half and Quarter Rupee of Victoria. 4 pieces
1753 UNCIRCULATED Cent of 1820, Colonial Coppers, Medals and Coins. 4 pieces

www.ingramcontent.com/pod-product-compliance
Lightning Source LLC
Chambersburg PA
CBHW020323090426
42735CB00009B/1377